English for Academic Study

New edition

Reading

Course Book

John Slaght

University of **Reading**

Garnet
EDUCATION

Credits

Published by
Garnet Publishing Ltd
8 Southern Court
South Street
Reading RG1 4QS, UK

This edition first published 2012.

Reprinted 2013, 2014, 2016.

ISBN: 978-1-90861-437-7

British Library Cataloguing-in-Publication Data
A catalogue record for this book is available from the British Library.

Production

Project manager:	Sarah MacBurnie
Project consultant:	Fiona McGarry
Editorial team:	Kayleigh Buller, Fiona Dempsey, Amanda Ilic, Kate Kemp
Art director:	Mike Hinks
Design and layout:	Simon Ellway, Maddy Lane, Ian Lansley
Photography:	Alamy, Corbis, iStockphoto

Printed and bound in Lebanon by International Press: interpress@int-press.com

The author and publishers wish to acknowledge the following use of material:

Billings, M. (2005). *The influenza pandemic of 1918*. Retrieved June 10, 2011, from Stanford University, Human Virology at Stanford website: http://stanford.edu/uda/

Brewer, S. (2008). *The SQ3R reading and study system*. Unpublished manuscript, International Study and Language Institute, University of Reading, UK.

Cattey, W. D. (2005). *The Tipping Point, by Malcolm Gladwell*: Book Review by Bill Cattey. Retrieved April 21, 2011, from http://web.mit.edu/wdc/www/tipping-point.html

Clarke, J. I., & Craven, A. (2006). Growing grey. *Geography Review, 2*(2), 10–13. Reproduced by permission of Philip Allan Updates.

Fletcher, K. (2008). *Sustainable fashion and textiles*. London: Earthscan. Retrieved June 6, 2011, from www.earthscan.co.uk.Portals/0/Files/Sample%20 Chapters/9781844074815.pdf. Reprinted with kind permission of Earthscan.

Gladwell, M. (2004). *Q&A with Malcolm: What is the Tipping Point?* [promotional interview]. Retrieved April 21, 2011, from www.gladwell.com/tippingpoint/index.html

Gladwell, M. (2010). *The Tipping Point: How Little Things Can Make a Big Difference*. London: Abacus.

Godfray, H. C. J., Beddington, J. R., Crute, I. R., Haddad, L., Lawrence, D., Muir, J. F., et al. (2010). The challenge of feeding 9 billion people. *Science, 327*(5967), 812–818.

Heathfield, S. M. (2011). What is human resource management? *About.com*. Retrieved July 9, 2011, from http://humanresources.about.com/od/glossaryh/f/hr_management.htm

Marsden, P. (2000). Mental epidemics. *New Scientist, 166*(2237), 46. Retrieved May 9, 2011, from www.newscientist.com/article/mg16622375.000-mental-epidemics.html. Reprinted with kind permission of *New Scientist*.

Parkinson, S., & Langley, C. (2009). Stop selling out science to commerce. *New Scientist, 204*(2733), 32–33. Reprinted with kind permission of *New Scientist*.

Price, A. (2007). *Human resource management in a business context*. (3rd ed.) (pp. 4–9). London: Thomson Learning. Reproduced by permission of Cengage Learning.

Rosenthal, E. (2010, December 11). Using waste, Swedish city cuts its fossil fuel. *The New York Times*. Retrieved May 9, 2011, from www.nytimes.com/2010/12/11/science/earth/11fossil.html. From *The New York Times*, December 11, 2010. © *The New York Times*. All rights reserved. Used by permission and protected by the Copyright Laws of the United States. The printing, copying, redistribution, or retransmission of the Material without express written permission is prohibited.

Scullion, H. (2005). International human resource management: An introduction. In H. Scullion, & M. Linehan (Eds.). (2005). *International human resource management: A critical text* (pp. 3–10). Basingstoke/New York: Palgrave Macmillan.

Sigman, A. (2009). Well connected? The biological implications of 'social networking'. *The Biologist 56*(1), 14–20. Reprinted with kind permission of the Society of Biology.

Smal, D. (2009, September). *The future of eco-fashion: A design-driven approach*. Paper presented at Fashion: Exploring Critical Issues (1st Global Conference), Oxford. Reprinted with kind permission of the author.

Sustainable fashion. (2010). *Intelligent Life*, Winter. Retrieved May 19, 2011, from http://moreintelligentlife.com/content/lifestyle/intelligent-life/sceptical-shopper-sustainable-fashion. © The Economist Newspaper Limited, London (2010).

tutor2u. (2011). *Human resources management: Introduction*. Retrieved October 27, 2011, from http://www.tutor2u.net/business/people/hrm_introduction.htm

Contents

c

Acknowledgements

EAS: Reading has been produced with the help of many students and the encouragement of colleagues from the International Study and Language Institute at the University of Reading. I want to thank them all.

Elena, Soochul, Suttawan, Naser, Hamed, Yibing, Meixin, Minghan, Bingnan, Proyphon, Yu-Chin (Gina), Manel, Avgi and Omar, this book is particularly dedicated to you and the vital role you played in trialling the materials in their final stages.

My colleague, Sarah Brewer, has been an inspiration in encouraging me at every stage of the development of this book and helping me to choose topics and think long and critically about what should be included.

A final word for Ros Richards, whose dynamic leadership has really been the driving force behind the whole EAS series.

John Slaght, April 2012

Reference to Source Book texts

Book map

Unit	Skills focus
1 **Reading for academic purposes**	
Reading for academic purposes	■ Reading for general understanding ■ Reading for specific details ■ Paragraph reorganization ■ Inferring meaning from context ■ Identifying word class ■ Reading for a purpose ■ Recalling information ■ Highlighting information to aid recall ■ Practising effective reading habits ■ Reflection: Development of reading skills
The SQ3R reading and study system	■ Reading and mind mapping ■ Summarizing the SQ3R system
2 **Sustainable energy**	
Using waste, Swedish city cuts its fossil fuel use (1)	■ Short-answer questions: Checking understanding and recall ■ Synonyms and word classes: Practising word classification ■ Synonyms in sentences: Practice in using synonyms
Using waste, Swedish city cuts its fossil fuel use (2)	■ Short-answer questions: Checking understanding and recall ■ Differentiating between main ideas and supporting details ■ Ways of making notes ■ Creating mind maps ■ Summarizing in note form
3 **The business of science**	
Stop selling out science to commerce	■ Reading practice: Timing reading; identifying the writers' viewpoint ■ Practising short-answer questions: Developing text recall ■ Understanding rhetorical questions and identifying the thesis ■ Scanning and close reading practice ■ Reading recall, focusing on a specific question ■ Inferring meaning from context ■ Paragraph reorganization: Looking at the logic of the text ■ Text-referring words: Developing understanding
Is business bad for science?	■ Predicting text content: Reflecting on own views ■ Comparing texts and reading for detail ■ Scanning and close reading practice ■ Identifying and using reporting language (direct and indirect) ■ Understanding and using modifying language
4 **Society today**	
Growing grey	■ Considering the title and the introduction ■ Considering subheadings: Using them to assist understanding ■ Considering displayed information: Important details ■ Making notes from memory: Discussion ■ Writing a summary

Unit	Skills focus
Well connected? The biological implications of 'social networking'	■ Considering the title and abstract ■ Reading, making notes and drawing conclusions ■ Writing a summary
5 Food security	
Diet and sustainability key to feeding the world: A food security report	■ Surveying the text ■ Search reading: Practising fast, accurate reading ■ Identifying functions of the text; annotating text ■ Examining the writer's choice of language for emphasis; identifying meaning from context
The challenge of feeding 9 billion people	■ Understanding the focus task ■ Predicting specific content in a text ■ Identifying the main ideas ■ Addressing the focus task; note-making and discussion ■ Logic and language: Organizing paragraphs into a logical order ■ Working out meaning from context; considering word class
Closing the yield gap	■ Predicting the content of the text ■ Identifying the function of paragraphs ■ Annotating the text using the Cornell system ■ Asking questions about the text ■ Predicting the content of the text
Dealing with the situation	■ Identifying the main ideas in the text; matching headings to sections ■ Identifying and dealing with assumed knowledge ■ Making use of displayed information ■ Producing notes
6 Human resource management	
Background and origins of people management	■ Defining the topic; considering own ideas ■ Expanding definitions ■ Completing notes: Building background information ■ Vocabulary extension: Producing sentences to activate use of words ■ Developing ideas about the topic ■ Reading for general understanding: Considering section headings ■ Making use of the text: Simulate preparation for a group presentation ■ Identifying and summarizing key points ■ Main points and supporting ideas: Considering the function of sentences
International human resource management	■ Practising fast, accurate reading ■ Using research as evidence ■ Identifying the writer's purpose ■ Focus task: Preparing notes to support a writer's discussion

Unit	Skills focus
7 Sustainable fashion	
Material diversity	■ Pre-reading task: Reflection and discussion ■ Analyzing the title ■ Understanding the main ideas of the text: Matching headings to sections ■ Identifying functions of the text; practice in annotating text ■ Identifying the writer's purpose: Annotating text ■ Producing a selective summary: Scanning text and selecting ideas
Sustainable fashion	■ Short-answer questions: Identifying main and supporting ideas ■ Finding supporting information
The future of eco-fashion: A design-driven approach	■ Analyzing the title ■ Working out meaning from context ■ Asking questions about the text ■ Reading for a purpose: Using annotation, summarizing ■ Dictionary work: Identifying words and definitions
8 The Tipping Point	
The Tipping Point: How Little Things Can Make a Big Difference	■ Selecting appropriate information ■ Reading and discussion; examining specific points
Mental epidemics	■ Pre-reading: Definitions ■ Identifying functions of the text ■ Reading for specific information ■ Unfamiliar words: Identifying word meaning from context and function ■ Identifying word class ■ Analyzing the writer's choice of expression ■ Writing a selective summary: Deconstructing a question
An interview with Malcolm Gladwell	■ Vocabulary: Identifying terms and discussion
***The Tipping Point* by Malcolm Gladwell: Book review**	■ Short-answer questions: Focusing on the text, discussion ■ Checking reading speed ■ Discussion: Improving reading strategies ■ Matching questions to sections in the text ■ Academic language: Examining text, reflection

Introduction

Aims of the course

The purpose of this book is to help you develop the academic reading skills you need to deal effectively with the reading and research you will need to carry out during your academic study. This course will particularly focus on reading for a specific academic purpose, working on effective reading strategies, detailed comprehension of sentences and paragraphs, and **text analysis**.

Structure of the course

Unit structure: There are eight units in the book. Each unit explores a key aspect of reading, such as *Considering the title and abstract*, and teaches it in the context of a specific topic area, e.g., *Growing grey*. You will have the opportunity to read texts on these and other topics in a separate Source Book. The reading tasks in any unit will be based on the unit topic.

Key reading skills: These are introduced where it is felt you need specific information on an area of reading. They usually appear at the end of a task and can be referred to either before you start the task, during the task, or when you have completed it.

Study tips: These are included for ease of reference when you are revising what you have studied. They either summarize the outcome of a series of activities or are a summary of other information contained in the unit.

Unit summary: Each unit is followed by a unit summary, giving you the opportunity to reflect on what you have learnt.

Additional material

Glossary: Words or phrases in **bold** in the text (or **bold** and <u>underlined</u> in the task instructions) are explained in the glossary on pages 110–111.

Working with the course

When you are reading in another language, you not only need to deal with the vocabulary and grammatical aspects of the text, but also understand the writing conventions associated with it. This can be particularly challenging with academic texts where the written conventions are even more important. The book will help you in two ways by:

- providing you with guided instruction on how to understand the structure of academic text
- giving you the opportunity to practise reading in a similar context to the one you will use in your future studies

What you put into the course will determine how much you get out of it. Obviously, if you want to improve your academic reading, it is essential to practise the skill. You should therefore prepare well for the sessions, as well as participating actively in them.

Course aims:

1 Reading for a specific academic purpose

This will help you find the relevant information in written sources that will help you complete an academic task. For example, you may need to:

- **combine information from a variety of sources** in order to complete an assignment on a specific question
- **research a new topic for an introductory overview** in order to assist with listening to a series of lectures on that topic
- **add new knowledge to what you already know about a topic** in order to carry out a variety of functions; add to your general understanding of a topic, write about your specialist area of interest, take notes for future exam revision, etc.

2 Working on effective reading strategies

The main strategies you will be looking at are:

a. Skimming

This involves looking at a text *quickly* for one of the following purposes:
- identifying what the text is about (the topic)
- identifying the main idea of the text
- deciding how useful the text is for your purposes
- deciding how you will make use of the text

Skimming a text might involve looking at some or all of the following features of the text:
- title
- section headings
- abstract or summary provided by the writer
- first and last paragraphs
- first and last sentences of intervening paragraphs
- **topic sentences** in each paragraph (see also Glossary: **paragraph leaders**)

Another form of skimming is when you are **previewing** a book to decide how useful it is for your purposes. In this situation, you might also look at one or more of the following:
- information about the author and/or publication details
- contents page
- **foreword** and/or introduction
- index

b. Predicting

This means using what you already know about the topic, what you want to learn about the topic from the text, and what you have learnt from your previewing, to guess what kind of information the text will contain and *how useful* it will be. You will be surprised how much you already know about a text before you even begin reading. Brainstorming your **prior knowledge** will help you to understand the text.

c. Scanning

This involves *finding words* (or other symbols, such as figures) that have particular importance for you. When you are scanning, you already know the form of the words or symbols you are looking for. When you scan, you normally focus on small parts of the text only.

d. Search reading

This involves quickly finding *ideas* that are important for you. This is different from scanning, because you don't know the exact words you are looking for in advance and cannot make a direct match.

e. Identifying the main ideas

This involves understanding the writer's *main points*. It may be possible to do this quite quickly after skimming the text. However, with more difficult texts, it may only be possible to identify the main ideas after more detailed reading.

f. Careful reading

This involves reading *slowly and carefully* so that you have a clear understanding of the text (or the part of the text that you are most interested in). You might do this in order to understand the *details* of the text or to **infer** *meaning* that is not directly stated (see g. below).

g. Inferring

This involves obtaining meaning from the text that the writer has *not explicitly stated*. Sometimes the writer expects you to fill gaps in the text for it to make sense. Sometimes you may wish to infer *why the author wrote the text*, i.e., the writer's purpose, and also the writer's attitude to what he/she is writing about.

h. Dealing with unfamiliar words

When you find a word you don't understand in a text, you first need to decide whether it is *necessary* to understand the word. Perhaps you can understand enough of the text without understanding the word – in which case you can ignore it. Alternatively, the context in which the word is located may allow you to guess the meaning of the word well enough to continue reading. If neither of these applies, you may have to look up the word in a dictionary. If you find you are using a dictionary so much that you cannot read the text at a reasonable speed, the text may be too specialized for you; in this case you should consider finding another one which deals with the same topic in a more generalized way.

An approach to dealing with new vocabulary is to decide whether you:

- need to know the word now to help you understand the text and use it later under different circumstances. In this case, you will need some way of recording the word, e.g., in a vocabulary notebook. You will also have to decide whether to rely on working out the meaning of the word from context, or whether you need to check in a dictionary.

- only need to know the word now to help you understand the text. This is often the case with technical words or low-frequency words; these are words that are not often used in English, even by native speakers of the language, except for specialist reasons. Of course, if you are reading a text in your academic area, you will need to know certain specialist vocabulary. You will need to record this vocabulary as well as use it so it becomes part of your **active vocabulary**, i.e., words that you use to communicate effectively.

- don't need to know this word either now or in the future. If the word does not prevent you from understanding the rest of the text, you probably do not need to worry about it. If the word occurs several times, however, you may feel it is necessary to work out its meaning or look it up and record it.

3 Detailed comprehension of sentences and paragraphs

In an academic context, much of your reading work will involve dealing with complete texts and extracting information from them in various ways, i.e., reading purposefully in order to make use of *content*. However, in order to fulfil your reading purpose, you may sometimes find it necessary to have a very precise understanding of specific sentences and paragraphs. There may be obstacles to your understanding in terms of grammar or ideas, or the text's organization or a combination of these. This is one area the course will help you solve.

Detailed comprehension involves analyzing the relationship between ideas within a specific sentence or between a sequence of sentences of up to paragraph length – or even beyond. This precise knowledge might be required, for example, to infer meaning, to view the content critically, to enhance overall understanding or to formulate precise understanding.

4 Text analysis

It is often helpful to understand the way a text is organized in order to make the best use of the information it contains. The organization of a text can be considered at the global level; for example, the way that the text is organized into sections and paragraphs according to the purpose of the text and the type of text. In a report of an experiment, for example, it is very common to see the pattern of organization on page 12.

- title
- abstract
- introduction/background
- methods
- results
- conclusions
- **references**/bibliography

Another aspect of organization that can be useful to examine is how information is organized logically at the local level, i.e., within **complex sentences** or paragraphs.

As you have seen, there are many different aspects of academic reading that you will consider during the course. Although it is important to be aware of all these different aspects, it is also important to:

- **develop a flexible reading style**. Becoming a better academic reader is not just about mastering different aspects of reading. It is also important to decide which is the best way to read a text, depending on the particular academic purpose that you have for reading it.
- **remember that the more you read, the better you will read**. Regular independent reading outside the classroom is essential for any student wishing to develop reading abilities such as fluency, greater reading speed, vocabulary acquisition and the strategies associated with successful reading.

You can improve your academic reading level by making decisions about:

- **why** you are reading
- **what** you are reading
- **how** you are reading
- **how well** you are reading

1 Reading for academic purposes

In this unit you will:

- practise and review the reading strategies outlined in the introduction
- develop strategies for deciding whether a text is useful
- build vocabulary through reading
- identify the organization of a text

Text	Reading for academic purposes, Text 1a (Source Book pp. 4–6)

Text 1a contains information on how to read for academic purposes more effectively.

Task 1	Reading for general understanding

The exercise below will give you practice in reading for general understanding. It is therefore important that you do not stop to look up any of the unknown words (you will get a fuller understanding of difficult vocabulary while completing some of the later tasks). The text in the Source Book consists of six sections. The table below contains seven headings that are possible summaries of the content for each section.

1.1 **Read the instructions below.**

a. Read the summary headings and underline the most important word or words in each one. If necessary, your teacher will explain the meaning of the language used.

b. Read Section 1 of the text and label the appropriate summary heading in the table.

Note: You will not use one of the headings.

c. Discuss your answer with other students and/or your teacher.

Study tip

Reading for general meaning is a very important skill that will help you deal with the amount of reading at university. See **skimming** in the Introduction, page 10.

Summary headings	Section
Linking effective reading to vocabulary acquisition	
Reading widely and **critically**	
Good reasons for reading	
The difficulties of reading academic texts	
The motivation behind reading	
Acquiring good reading habits	
The EAP reading syllabus	

1.2   **Now read and match Sections 2–6 to the appropriate summary headings in the table.**

Note: One of the summary headings does not need to be used.

| Task 2 | **Reading for specific details** |

2.1   **Read Text 1a again and find the answers to the following questions.**

You will use some of your answers to complete another task later in the unit.

Study tip

Being able to read for specific detail is another important skill. See **scanning**, **search reading** and **careful reading** on pages 10–11 of the Introduction.

1. What type of reading material is Bassett (2010) concerned with?

_____

2. Bassett believes the key to the best understanding of a text is …

_____

3. The greater the reader's reading ability, the greater their …

_____

4. What are the two main criteria for text selection for an EAP course?

_____

5. When are EAP students more likely to read subject-related material?

_____

6. What does a critical reader use to assess the value of a text?

_____

7. What is Kurland's main idea?

_____

8. What helps to determine how a text should be read?

_____

9. What reason for reading is suggested for students in higher education?

_____

10. How much daily reading is recommended?

_____

11. What are all the words that an individual knows in a language called?

_____

12. What are postgraduates often given before starting their studies?

_____

13. How much exposure to a word is needed before its use becomes automatic?

_____

Task 3	**Paragraph reorganization**

The second paragraph of Section 6 has been removed from the original text in the Source Book. The sentences from the removed paragraph are listed below, but they are in the wrong order.

3.1 **Read the sentences and arrange them in the appropriate order to form a paragraph.**
  a. Read sentences 2 and 3 that have been identified as the first and final sentences.
  b. Read sentences 1, 4, 5 and 6 and identify the correct order.
  c. Complete the remaining boxes with the appropriate number.

  1. This is one of the reasons why most reached university level in their home countries. ☐

  2. Fluency in both written and spoken language will only develop with practice. ☐ 1

  3. Thus, the more students work on developing good reading habits, the more fluent they should become and the more successful they are likely to be in their academic studies. ☐ 6

  4. Nonetheless, university students are expected to read a considerable amount during a typical week. ☐

  5. In fact, international students studying through English are normally already fluent readers in their own languages. ☐

  6. International academics, i.e., students, have to do this in a foreign language – English. ☐

Task 4	**Inferring meaning from context**

Not knowing the meaning of words is one of the main difficulties faced by language learners reading in a foreign language. When you come across a word which is unfamiliar, try to avoid automatically reaching for a dictionary or tapping the word into your electronic translator; develop the habit of reading on in the text to see if this helps your understanding. If, however this does not help, experiment with the following advice.

4.1 **Look at the sentence from Text 1a and discuss the meaning of the underlined word with another student. If this word was new to you, what helped you <u>infer</u> its meaning?**

> Bassett's focus is on graded readers, but <u>arguably</u> the type of text should suit the needs and interests of individuals.

Key reading skills: Inferring meaning

One way of identifying the meaning of the word is to look at it in context – the way it is used within the sentence. For example, in the sentence above, the word *but* is used to indicate a contrast or difference. Thus, although Bassett is interested in graded readers, the writer is saying there is *arguably* more to reading than just readers. In other words, there is some sort of *argument* or *disagreement* involved.

Another way is to think of the 'root' word, which in this case is *argue* – which means 'to not agree about something.'

You might also think about words with a similar sound or spelling which may help you. The key thing is that the more you think about a word, the more likely it is to become part of your active lexicon.

It is also useful to recognize and understand the way that language varies within a text. One way of varying language is through the use of *synonyms*.

A synonym is a word or phrase that has the same meaning, or almost the same meaning, as another word or phrase.

4.2 **Read Section 1 again from Text 1a and find synonyms for the words in the left-hand column. There is an example in the first row.**

Defining words	Synonym	Line number
proof/confirmation	*evidence*	7
a wide range of		
closely connected/significant		
get something back		
help/make easier		
without being aware of or without thinking about something		
ability/skill		
something which is aimed at or is the main focus		

Task 5	Identifying word class

5.1 **Read the following definitions of <u>word classes</u> and match them to the correct word in the box.**

Note: Identifying the word class of a word or phrase often helps you to work out the meaning of a word you don't know.

> conjunction   preposition   noun   adverb   verb   adjective   pronoun

1. a word referring to a person, a place or a thing _____

2. an action or doing word _____

3. a word that describes what a person, a place or a thing is like _____

4. a word used to describe a verb, an adjective or another adverb _____

5. a word which comes before a noun or a pronoun and shows its relation to another part of the sentence _____

6. a word that is used to replace a person, a place or a thing _____

7. a word that is used to join other words, phrases, clauses or sentences _____

5.2 **Read Sections 2–5 from Text 1a and find the words in the table. Complete the table by writing the line number where each word occurs in the text and the word class of each word. The first one has been done for you.**

Word/phrase	Line number	Word class
topics	31	noun
typically		
this		
blends		
consideration		
simply		
through		
embark		
their		
only		

5.3   **Look at the words from Ex 5.2 and choose which ones you want to record.**

You should record words if:

- you don't know their meaning or how they are used, and/or
- you think they might be useful words to know either now or for future academic purposes

Key reading skills: Choosing and recording new words from a text

One way of deciding which words to record is to check how frequently the word is used by native speakers. You can do this by visiting the *Compleat Lexical Tutor*, which can be found at www.lextutor.ca/vp/bnc; here you will find that, for example, the adverb *arguably* is a K1 word – in other words, it is among the 1,000 most commonly used words. Considering this information, you may decide that it is a word you would want to use in future and, therefore, keep a record of.

Task 6	Reading for a purpose

At various stages in Units 1–8, you will be given a Focus task. This is an essay question, or similar academic task, that is linked to a reading text or texts in the Source Book. The Focus task will help direct your reading and the use you make of the text(s) to **synthesize** ideas.

FOCUS TASK 👁

> Summarize the main points of the text 'Reading for academic purposes'.

6.1   **Re-read Text 1a and then write a short one-paragraph summary of the main ideas. You can use some of the answers in Task 2 to help you.**

Key reading skills: Reading selectively

At university level, you may be given extensive reading lists. It can be a daunting prospect to read all the texts and sources and to understand them at the same time. It is therefore important to **read selectively**. This means thinking carefully about your reading purpose and concentrating only – or mainly – on texts, or parts of texts, which are relevant to that reading purpose.

Task 7	Recalling information

Do you think reading is a very important language skill?

Even if you read selectively, you may still have a considerable amount of text to *read*, *understand* and ***recall***. This has to be achieved as quickly and as effectively as possible. The following tasks aim to help you recall and use information from an academic text.

7.1   **Re-read Section 1 from Text 1a, straight through without stopping or checking for meaning in a dictionary. Then follow instructions a–c to find out how much information you can recall.**

a.   Put the text away and write down in note form (words or phrases) anything you can remember about the information you have just read.

b.   Compare your notes with another student to see to what extent you have 'recalled' the same information. Decide whether there are any gaps in your notes.

c.   Check the text and add any further notes you think are useful to summarize the main idea(s) in this section.

7.2   **Re-read Section 2. This time, underline or highlight main points as you read. Again, read without stopping or using a dictionary. Read only once.**

a.   Put the text away and recall in note form (words or phrases) anything you can remember about the information you have just read.

b.   Compare your notes with the original text. Have you 'recalled' the text more effectively this time? If so, why do you think this is?

Now read through Sections 3 and 4 without stopping or using a dictionary. Recall these two sections in the same way.

7.3   **Decide whether you found underlining or highlighting more effective. Discuss your conclusions with another student.**

7.4   **Carefully consider the following question:**

> How can readers independently develop effective reading habits?

Tell another student what you think the answer is.

7.5   **Re-read Sections 5 and 6, then follow steps a–d to find an answer to the question in Ex 7.4.**

You can underline or highlight key words or ideas if you think this is useful.

a.   Copy down the question in Ex 7.4.

b.   Put away the text and from memory make notes that might help you answer the question.

c.   Check the text for accuracy and make any necessary amendments to your notes.

d.   Finally, using the notes for Sections 5 and 6, briefly summarize your answer to the question in Ex 7.4.

Task 8   Reflection

8.1   **How did reading and making notes at the same time affect your reading? Choose one or more of the expressions below and/or write your own brief comment explaining your reaction to the exercises in Task 7.**

It made reading and understanding:

a.   slower

I found reading and understanding slower because I had to decide which parts of the text were main ideas and make suitable notes.

b. quicker

_____

_____

c. less laborious

_____

_____

d. more purposeful

_____

_____

e. less interesting

_____

_____

f. annoying

_____

_____

Add your own ideas:

_____

_____

Text	The SQ3R reading and study system, Text 1b (Source Book p. 7)

Text 1b contains information on a particular study system you can use to improve academic reading.

Task 9	Reading and mind mapping

You are going to practise reading and recording information on a mind map. You will also check your reading speed; this is to encourage you to read *fast*, an essential first step to effective reading.

9.1 **Read Text 1b carefully, but as fast as you can.**
Before you start reading, note the time. When you finish reading, note the time again.

9.2 **Complete the mind map without referring back to the text.**
Complete as many of the circles as you can with the appropriate word and fill in the underlined gaps.

Mind map of SQ3R

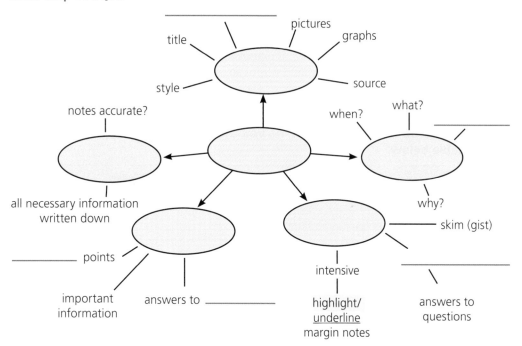

9.3 **Discuss your mind map with another student and amend or complete it as necessary.**

This is an important step in the process. You will find that when you *discuss* your understanding of the text you will remember more than you first thought.

9.4 **Check your mind map against the text for accuracy.**

Calculating your reading speed

The text has 621 words. Divide this number by the number of minutes it took you to read the text. This will give you your reading speed. Even though you have tried to read fast, you will probably discover that you have understood more of the text than you expected, especially after discussing with a partner. If this is not the case, your understanding will improve over time. Your target is at least 75 per cent understanding.

The average native speaker of English can read between 200 and 250 words per minute when reading quickly.

Task 10	**Summarizing the SQ3R system**

10.1 **Using your mind map, write a brief summary of the SQ3R system.**

10.2 **Compare your summary with that of another student and discuss any differences.**

Unit summary

The checklists at the end of each unit are intended to help you reflect on the work you have covered. They will help you decide to what extent you feel you have progressed with the activities and skills covered. A number of activities have been introduced in the first unit of the book. These are listed below.

1 **Look back over the work you have done and think about how successfully you carried out the various tasks. As you check, tick (✔) the appropriate box in the table below.**

Skills	very well	quite well	need more work	not covered
Reading for general understanding				
Reading for specific details				
Identifying paragraph organization				
Inferring meaning from context				
Identifying word classes				
Reading for a purpose				
Rapid and efficient reading				
Recalling and highlighting information				
Experimenting with reading methods				
Using a mind map and SQ3R				

2 **Complete the following.**

a. 'Word class' means

_____

b. Highlighting or underlining can be used to

_____

c. SQ3R stands for

_____

d. A mind map can be used for

_____

For web resources relevant to this book, see:
www.englishforacademicstudy.com
These weblinks will provide you with comprehensive information on how to develop effective reading strategies and skills, and how to understand the differences between conventional and academic reading.

2 Sustainable energy

In this unit you will:

- identify synonyms and word classes
- differentiate between main ideas and supporting points

| Text | Using waste, Swedish city cuts its fossil fuel use (1), Text 2a
(Source Book pp. 8–9) |

Text 2a contains information about the Swedish city of Kristianstad, which uses waste for the purposes of heating. You will use the text to write a summary of the ways fossil fuel use has been reduced.

Task 1 Short-answer questions

1.1 **Read for specific information.**

a. Study the questions for three minutes.

b. Close your Course Book. Read Text 2a carefully, but as fast as you can. Time yourself to see how long it takes you.

c. Close your Source Book and answer as many questions as you can.

1. Twenty years ago, Kristianstad got its heating from:
   a. biomass
   b. solar panels
   c. fossil fuels
   d. wind turbines

2. What is Kristianstad's main industry?
   a. waste processing
   b. alcohol production
   c. food production
   d. alternative energy production

3. Which <u>two</u> of the following are <u>not</u> mentioned as ingredients for generating energy?
   a. used cooking oil
   b. rotting fruit
   c. potato peels
   d. manure
   e. stale bread

4. In which area of Kristianstad is the energy-generating plant situated?

5. Which one of the following is used as a local source of power in Kristianstad?
   a. rivers
   b. landfill
   c. lakes
   d. alcohol

6. What energy source are most European countries investing in?

   _____

7. What is a major source of renewable energy in agricultural areas?

   _____

8. By what amount has Kristianstad reduced its fossil fuel use?
   a. a half
   b. a quarter
   c. three-quarters
   d. one-third

9. How many biomass digesters exist in the United States?
   a. 1,800
   b. 151
   c. 8,000
   d. 1,550

10. What are the two Southern California utility companies planning to do?
    a. buy up farmland
    b. build biogas plants
    c. take over another utility company
    d. open water treatment plants

1.2 **Check your answers with another student.**
This step has been included to encourage you to discover how much you understand even when reading fast. You will find you remember more than you think when you discuss your answers.

1.3 **Check your answers against Text 2a.**
Record the number of questions you answered correctly.

1.4 **Calculate your reading speed.**
Divide the number of words in the text (566) by the number of minutes it took you to read the text.

Key reading skills: Improving your reading speed
It can be hard to read academic texts quickly, but you can improve your reading speed with regular, timed reading practice. Make a mental note of what helps you to read quickly. This may include: the layout of the text, headings and visuals and even the time of day you read.

Task 2   Synonyms and word classes

In Unit 1, you looked at how to infer the meaning of new words in a text. In Text 2a there are a number of useful words and phrases that you may not be familiar with.

2.1   **Find words or phrases in the text with the same, or similar, meaning to the words or phrases in the left-hand column of the table below.**

Complete the table by adding the relevant word class and the synonym from the text.

Word	Line number	Synonym in text	Word class
detach from something	2	to wean from	verb
ambition/hope			
icy cold			
a turnaround/change			
replaced			
accumulation of rubbish			
exploiting/making use of			
extremely important			
to be in charge of something			
create/set up			
achieve what is necessary			

2.2   **Use the synonyms you have found to complete the following sentences.**

Note: You may need to change the form of the word.

1. The dramatic drop in temperature resulted in _____ conditions throughout the country.

2. Current research into animal behaviour is being _____ by an emeritus professor of zoology.

3. A new suite of PCs has been _____ in one of the seminar rooms at the university.

4. The identification of the parasite causing malaria was _____ in efforts to overcome this terrible disease.

5. The new prime minister's victory in the elections was a complete _____ of the defeat he suffered the previous time.

2.3   Now write sentences of your own to help you remember some of the other words in Ex 2.1.

2.4   Compare your sentences with those of another student.

Text	Using waste, Swedish city cuts its fossil fuel use (2), Text 2b (Source Book pp. 10–11)

Text 2b contains information on how Kristianstad has managed to harness waste to heat the city.

Task 3	Short-answer questions

3.1   **Read for specific information.**

a.   Study the multiple-choice questions for three minutes.

b.   Close your Course Book. Read Text 2b carefully, but as fast as you can. Time yourself as before.

c.   Close your Source Book and answer the questions. You may wish to discuss your answers before checking them against the text.

   1.   Biogas is essentially:
      a.   natural gas
      b.   biological waste
      c.   non-renewable
      d.   heat-trapping

   2.   The Bioenergy Initiative is based in:
      a.   Wisconsin
      b.   Sweden
      c.   California
      d.   Germany

   3.   From one greenhouse alone, how much CO_2 has been eliminated by the use of wood pellets?
      a.   24 tons
      b.   64 tons
      c.   84 tons
      d.   104 tons

   4.   Using biogas to heat municipal buildings saves Kristianstad:
      a. $3.2 million per year
      b. $114 million per year
      c. $70 million per year
      d. $3.8 million per year

   5.   The Kristianstad council makes money by:
      a.   selling excess diesel
      b.   spending less on electricity
      c.   charging money for waste disposal
      d.   reducing the heating level

6. When did Kristianstad start its energy conversion project?
   a. the 1960s
   b. the 1970s
   c. the 1980s
   d. the 1990s

7. Where is the 'district heating system' located?
   a. under the ground
   b. in hospitals
   c. in schools
   d. around the city

8. What action was taken in Sweden in 1991?
   a. a switch to a new heating system
   b. a tax on CO_2 emissions
   c. the installation of a biogas plant
   d. a ban on wood burning

9. What is the Swedish government doing to promote pellet-fuelled heating?
   a. selling it to farmers
   b. exporting it to Europe
   c. building furnaces
   d. providing it cheaply

10. By 2020, Kristianstad city planners hope to:
    a. build a new biogas plant
    b. reduce fossil fuel emissions
    c. run municipal vehicles on biogas
    d. have no polluting emissions

Key reading skills: Fast reading
Fast readers read in 'chunks'. This means you should try to read whole phrases, rather than looking at each word separately. This will take practice, as you first have to change a reading habit; in time, reading in chunks will become your new reading habit.

3.2 Check your answers against the text.
Record the number of questions you answered correctly. Did you score higher than in Task 1?

| Task 4 | Differentiating between main ideas and supporting details |

In Unit 1, you were introduced to **reading for a purpose**, i.e., concentrating on the texts or parts of texts that are relevant to your reading purpose. Your reading purpose now is to identify main ideas.

4.1 Re-read Text 2b and study the information in sentences 1–6 below.
a. Find the relevant sections of the text.
b. Select three pieces of information which are main ideas.
   1. Tanker trucks are now being used for delivering wood pellets.
   2. Both old fossil fuel technologies and a modern biomass replacement exist in Kristianstad.
   3. Natural gas and biogas are polluting when burnt, but much less than coal and oil.
   4. The policy director of the Wisconsin group describes biomass as an 'opportunity fuel'.

5. Kristianstad no longer uses fossil fuels and is now making use of other sources of energy.
6. New York also uses a district heating system.

Key reading skills: Differentiating main ideas from supporting details

In an academic context, it is important to be able to extract the main ideas from a text, particularly if the text contains complex ideas and a lot of supporting points. A paragraph generally contains one main idea and may have several supporting details. You first need to identify the main points and extract the key information. You can then decide which of the supporting details are also relevant to your reading purpose.

Study tip

The key reading skills in this unit are particularly useful for increasing your reading speed and understanding.

Task 5	**Ways of making notes**

One effective way of making notes is to draw a mind map.

5.1   **Look at paragraph 1 of Text 2b and complete the mind map below.**

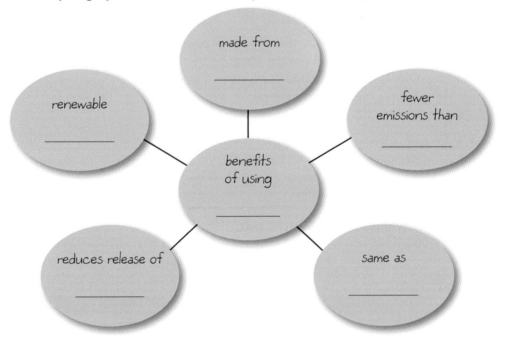

Task 6	**Creating mind maps**

6.1   **After reading the text and highlighting the main ideas, study the mind map on the next page and then complete the blanks.**

6.2   **Identify which information in the mind map seems the most useful, and which seems irrelevant.**

Note: You may be able to use some of the information in the mind map to write the first draft of your summary.

6.3   **Check the text to identify any further information that could be added to the mind map.**

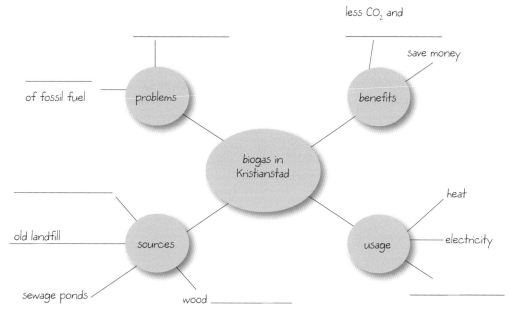

less CO_2 and _____

save money

_____
of fossil fuel   problems   benefits

biogas in
Kristianstad

heat

old landfill   sources   usage   electricity

sewage ponds   wood _____   _____

Task 7	**Summarizing in note form**

You are going to use both Texts 2a and 2b to write a brief summary.

FOCUS TASK 👁

▶   How has Kristianstad cut its fossil fuel use?

7.1   **Re-read both texts once.**
   a.   Put the texts away and write down in note form everything you can remember that is relevant to the Focus task question.
   b.   Compare your notes with another student's. Decide whether there are any gaps in your notes.
   c.   Check the texts to add any further notes or to make any amendments.
   d.   Draw your own mind map to display the key points of your notes.

7.2   **Using only your notes and mind map, write your summary.**
   Your summary should be no more than 120 words.

Unit summary

Some new activities have been introduced in this second unit. You have also had further practice in some activities that were introduced in Unit 1.

1 **Look back over the work you have done and think about how successfully you carried out the various tasks. As you check, tick (✔) the appropriate box in the table below.**

Skills and techniques	very well	quite well	need more work	not covered
Developing fast, efficient reading				
Identifying word classes				
Identifying and using synonyms				
Differentiating between main and supporting points				
Summarizing in note form				

2 **Read the following definition of the word *synonym*. Then complete the following sentences containing the word *synonymous* with an appropriate association. You may find that your ideas differ from other students.**

A *synonym* can be defined as a word or phrase that means exactly or nearly the same as another word or phrase in the same language, for example 'near' is a synonym of 'close'. It is also said that a synonym is a person or thing so closely associated with a particular quality or idea that the mention of their name calls it to mind; for example, the British royal family is *synonymous with British tradition and culture*.

Example: Examinations are synonymous with *hard work, worry and nerves*.

1. Soft toys are synonymous with _____.

2. Manufacturers hope that their products will become synonymous with _____

    _____.

3. Diamonds are synonymous with _____.

4. Punctuality is synonymous with _____.

5. Sports and games are synonymous with _____.

For web resources relevant to this book, see:
www.englishforacademicstudy.com
These weblinks will provide you with information about developing your pre-reading strategies and further information on how to read effectively.

3 The business of science

In this unit you will:

- handle rhetorical questions and identify the thesis
- quickly identify the main points of the text
- infer meaning from context
- identify and use reporting language and modifying language

Text	Stop selling out science to commerce, Text 3a (Source Book pp. 12–13)

Text 3a is an article from *New Scientist* on how commercial pressure influences scientific research.

Task 1 | Fast reading

1.1 **Read Text 3a to get a general understanding of the content.**
Read as quickly as you can to get a general idea of the text. Note the time before you begin reading and note it again when you have finished. There are 854 words in the text.

1.2 **When you have finished reading the text, tick (✔) the statement you think most closely reflects the writers' point of view.**

1. Governments should give more support to universities. ☐

2. Researchers should avoid involvement with commercial or military interests. ☐

3. Academic research should be carried out with an open mind. ☐

4. Universities must only serve the interests of the general public. ☐

Task 2 | Short-answer questions

2.1 **Re-read the text and try to answer the following questions from memory.**
Answer as many questions as you can. Then check the text to find any other answers. Use no more than <u>seven</u> words to answer each question.

1. Which commercial sectors have been most criticized because of their harmful influences?

_____

2. Give one example of how universities are influenced by the commercial sector.

   _____

3. In what way are many universities linked to military interests?

   _____

4. What are the tobacco and oil industries particularly believed to be guilty of?

   _____

5. What is 'blue-sky' research?
   Research which:
   a. favours the commercial sector
   b. has no immediate commercial value
   c. is investigating global warming
   d. is not very important

6. Why is 'low-input' agriculture receiving very little scientific attention?

   _____

7. What other area linked to agricultural production is often neglected?

   _____

8. What phrase in Section 4 refers to various types of weapon?

   _____

9. Which academic institution is challenging the influence of the commercial sector?

   _____

10. What does 'SGR' stand for?

    _____

11. What final recommendation do the writers make?

    _____

12. What is the source of this text?

    _____

| Task 3 | Understanding rhetorical questions and identifying the thesis |

Text 3a consists of an introduction, four more sections and a conclusion. The first sentence of the introduction asks a question. This type of question is known as a rhetorical question, i.e., one that the writer goes on to answer.

3.1 **Re-read the opening summary paragraph and identify the rhetorical question.**
Choose the correct answer to the question.
1. Yes, they have a negative impact.
2. No, people are indifferent.
3. We are not sure of the answer.

3.2 **Complete the flow chart to identify the writers' thesis.**
There is no thesis statement in the text, but you can identify the thesis by picking out the key phrases.

1. _____

▼

2. _negative impact on science_ _____

▼

3. _____

▼

4. _cannot be ignored_ _____

3.3 **Write the thesis in one sentence below. Use your notes from the flow chart to help you.**

_____

_____

_____

3.4 **Compare your sentence with that of another student and discuss the differences.**

> **Study tip**
>
> Understanding the writer's thesis is a key element in understanding the text.

| Task 4 | Scanning and close reading practice |

4.1 **Look at Section 1 of Text 3a. Which of the following do you consider to be the best summary heading? Why?**
1. Huge industrial influence on research is a major problem.
2. Commercial interests in research have only short-term benefits.
3. Interference in research is limited to certain academic disciplines.

4.2 Re-read Section 2 and provide a suitable short title for the section. You can use a phrase from the text.

_____

_____

_____

4.3 Re-read Section 3. Which do you consider to be the best summary heading?
1. Governments always support commercial enterprise.
2. Short-term interests come first.
3. The public never benefits from research activities.

Explain your decision below.

_____

_____

_____

4.4 Re-read Section 4. What is the key point the writers make?
Sometimes it is not immediately clear what the writer's key point is. First, identify the topic of the section you are reading and then ask yourself: What is the writer saying about the topic?
1. Military interests come first in research activities.
2. Public interests are not being considered.
3. Scientists are manipulated by political interests.

4.5 Re-read the conclusion. What do the writers conclude? Summarize the key idea in no more than three words.

_____

_____

_____

Compare your ideas with another student.

Task 5	Focus task and reading recall

Remember that the Focus task will help direct your reading and the use you make of the text(s) to synthesize ideas.

FOCUS TASK 👁

▶ To what extent should academic research be supported by commercial interests and political decisions?

5.1   **Read and underline the key words in the Focus task. Then follow the steps.**

Step 1: Re-read the text and then put it away.

Step 2: Recall any information that would help you answer the Focus task question, writing short notes, phrases or even single words.

Step 3: Check your notes with other students.

Step 4: Write a summary in response to the Focus task question using your combined notes.

Task 6	Inferring meaning from context

6.1   **Study the phrases in the table below and identify them in Text 3a. Write the possible meaning of each one in the table.**
Try to work out their meaning by using the context in which you find them – without using a dictionary.

Phrase	Possible meaning	Line(s)
academic landscape		
commercial mindset		
conflicts of interest		
research is undermined		
cornerstone of science		
'blue-sky' research		
the roots of conflict		
becoming discomfited		
ethical standards		
to this end		
they could do worse than		

Check your ideas with another student.

Key reading skills: Word combinations
Familiar words are often combined into unfamiliar phrases in a new context. Remember to use your existing knowledge of the words and look for contextual and grammatical clues to guess the meaning of the unfamiliar phrases.

7.1 **In the following paragraph (extracted from Text 3a), the sentences are in the wrong order. Number the sentences to create a logical sequence.**

Make use of lexical clues to help you. Before you start, look at the final sentence of the previous paragraph.

> A new report from the organisation Scientists for Global Responsibility (SGR) exposes problems so serious that we can no longer afford to be indifferent to them.

1. We found a wide range of disturbing commercial influences on science, and evidence that similar problems are occurring across academic disciplines. ☐

2. But we also looked at the oil and gas, defence and biotech sectors, which have been subjected to less scrutiny. ☐

3. The damaging influence of two of these, pharmaceuticals and tobacco, has been noted before. ☐

4. The report looks at the impact of five commercial sectors on science and technology over the past 20 years. ☐

Now check your rearrangement against the original order in the text.

Task 8 | **Text-referring words**

8.1 **Look at the text to find the text-referring words in the table. Note down the idea or word(s) that each one refers to.**

Line	Text-referring word(s)	Refers to ...
33	This	most of the previous paragraph, i.e., the conflict between traditional academic and business-oriented research
38	they	
47	these tactics	
54	This	
87	them	
100	These	
109	them	
109	They	

Key reading skills: Understanding text-referring words
Text-referring words take their meaning from the surrounding text; they may refer back to words or ideas that have already been used, or forward to ideas that will be expanded on later in the text. They include pronouns, nouns and short phrases that refer to things and ideas that have already been mentioned. They therefore avoid the need for the author to keep repeating him/herself. It is important to be aware of the way that text-referring words clarify the progression of ideas and make the text more cohesive.

Text	Is business bad for science? Text 3b (Source Book pp. 14–16)

This text is based on an article from an online newsletter, *I-sis News,* which looks further into commercial pressure on scientific research.

Task 9	**Predicting text content**

Predicting the content of a text will help you read with more speed and fluency. It may also help you to identify the writer's purpose and to recognize 'new' knowledge.

9.1 **Think about the title: *Is business bad for science?***
a. Discuss why big business might equal bad science with another student.
b. Add four more reasons why business can be bad for science.

1. *pressure to complete research too quickly*

2. _____

3. _____

4. _____

5. _____

9.2 **Suggest one reason why science can be 'bad for business'?**

_____

_____

9.3 **Now read to see if your ideas were the same as those in Text 3b.**
While you are reading, you can also time yourself. Note the time before you begin reading and note it again when you have finished. There are 1,300 words in the text.

Study tip

Predicting involves using the knowledge you already have about a topic to help you understand a text you are going to read on that topic.

9.4   **Tick (✔) a statement that most closely reflects the writer's viewpoint.**

1. Scientific research needs to be carried out in a more businesslike way. ☐

2. The public is not gaining adequate benefit from research aimed at developing new drugs. ☐

3. There is a serious conflict between investors' interests and appropriate scientific practice. ☐

4. Scientists and universities have very limited commercial sense. ☐

Discuss your views.

Task 10	Comparing texts and reading for detail

You have now read two texts on the relationship between business and scientific research.

10.1   **Think about the two texts you have read on the same topic: the relationship between business and scientific research. Are there any significant differences between them?**
Summarize your answer and then explain it to another student.

10.2   **Re-read Text 3b and complete the short-answer questions.**

1. Which area of scientific research is the focus of this text?

    _____

2. Who were the delegates to the London conference in 2001?

    _____

3. Name the two sorts of research mentioned by Ziman.

    _____

4. Which type of research did Weatherall appear to favour?

    _____

5. How did Weatherall think that scientific research could be protected?

    _____

6. Why was Olivieri ethically opposed to certain research?

    _____

7. What term did Monbiot use to describe typical government attitudes to research?

    _____

8. Identify the phrase Monbiot used to demonstrate what he wanted scientists to do.

    _____

9. Who wrote the report about the London conference?

_____

10. What concern did Pisano express about science's relationship with business?

_____

10.3 **Select parts of the text that seem very similar to or very different from Text 3a.**
Note: You could use different colours to highlight 'similar' and 'different' information.

| Task 11 | **Scanning and close reading practice** |

Academic texts often contain references to experts within the relevant field. In Text 3b, the opinions of a number of academics and scientists are mentioned.

11.1 **Read the brief summaries below. Then scan the text for information, matching each opinion to the relevant expert.**

a. Select the experts in various areas from the following list: Pisano, Weatherall, Olivieri, Ziman, Monbiot, Saunders and Mae-Wan Ho. **Note:** In some cases, more than one expert may be linked to a summary.

b. Scan the text to find information which relates to the summaries below and complete the table.

1. Research institutions clearly need outside funding, but at the same time they need to guard against exploitation by business interests.

2. Only a few business enterprises have made significant financial gain from funding medical research.

3. Governments, businesses, institutions and scientists should all share some blame for conducting inappropriate scientific research.

4. Scientific research should serve the interests of society as a whole, not just the few.

5. Some drug companies are guilty of promoting medical malpractice by concealing the results of their funded research.

6. The biotech industry cannot be managed in the same way as other modern industries.

7. Funding of research is often misdirected in order to suit the aims of business or government interests.

Summary	Expert
1.	Weatherall
2.	
3.	
4.	
5.	
6.	
7.	

Task 12 Identifying and using reporting language

Academic texts often contain references to experts within the relevant field. In Text 3b, the opinions of a number of academics and scientists are mentioned.

The text contains an interesting range of reporting language. This is the way that the writer tells the reader, i.e., 'reports', what the various experts referred to in the text said or wrote about. The first speaker at the London conference who is reported in this way is Professor John Ziman. Note the various ways, in paragraph 5, in which the writer of the text reports Ziman's ideas:

1. *the late John Ziman … who categorized research as …* (lines 72–75)
2. *Ziman described instrumental …* (lines 85–86)
3. *Ziman noted that although non-instrumental …* (lines 93–94)
4. *Ziman argued that …* (line 104)

12.1   **It is important to recognize the different ways that Ziman's viewpoint is expressed in this paragraph. Look at the list of reporting language above and identify whether each one is direct or indirect reporting. Tick (✔) the appropriate column in the table below.**

	1.	2.	3.	4.
Direct				
Indirect				

Key reading skills: Identifying reporting language
Being able to identify reporting language will help you to read more effectively and will help you write academic texts such as essays, reports and dissertations.

12.2   **Read through the remainder of the text and highlight more examples of reporting language. You may be able to find up to 25 different examples in the complete text.**
Discuss these examples and decide which of them you might be able to use in your academic writing.

12.3   **Look back at the opinions of academics in Task 11. Using different reporting verbs, practise reporting what various experts said about scientific research.**
Try to avoid using the same verb as the one used in the original text.

Example: Weatherall *emphasized that* research institutions clearly needed outside funding, but at the same time, they needed to guard against exploitation by business interests.

| Task 13 | **Understanding and using modifying language** |

Adjectives and adverbs are used to modify or say more about other words in texts. They serve an important role in informing the reader about the writer's attitude, bias and overall writing purpose. They also perform an evaluative role so that the reader can critically consider the importance or relevance of certain ideas, opinions or facts.

Remember

Adjectives are used to modify nouns. **Example:** This is a *controversial* question.

Adverbs are used to modify verbs [1], adjectives [2] or other adverbs [3]. **Example:** She read *very* [3] *quickly* [1] through the *extremely* [2] long agenda.

13.1   **Re-read paragraphs 2 and 3 (lines 12–47) of Text 3b. Then complete the table with the words or phrases from the text that modify the words and phrases in the left-hand column.**

Consider how the modifying language helps you understand the text.

Word or phrase	Modifying language
1. The impact	*substantial*
2. demand	
3. return	
4. questions	
5. scientists and institutions	
6. business tactics	
7. serves	

13.2   **Re-read paragraph 5, (lines 72–108) and find seven more examples of the way adjectives and adverbs are used to modify other words.**

a.   Record the words and modifiers in the table.

b.   Consider what impact the modifying language in this paragraph has for the reader.

Word or expression	Modifying language
1.	
2.	
3.	
4.	
5.	
6.	
7.	

Unit summary

Some new activities have been introduced in this third unit. You have also had further practice in the skills and activities introduced in earlier units.

1 **Look back over the work you have done and think about how successfully you carried out the various tasks. As you check, tick (✔) the appropriate box in the table below.**

Skills and techniques	very well	quite well	need more work	not covered
Recalling text from memory				
Identifying the writer's thesis				
Scanning for specific ideas or information				
Inferring meaning from context				
Identifying the lexical and logical links in a paragraph				
Using previous knowledge to predict text content				
Identifying and putting reporting language into practice				
Identifying and using modifying language				

2 **Complete the following statements with phrases from the word box. You will not need one phrase.**

text-referring words	help to modify	a thesis statement outlines
reporting language refers to		a rhetorical question
understood a text		use your prior knowledge

a. The more you can recall, the more you will have _____.

b. _____ is one that the writer or speaker answers themselves.

c. _____ the argument, belief or claim made by the writer.

d. _____ link between words, names or concepts in a text.

e. In order to predict the content of a text, it is usually necessary to _____.

f. _____ statements made by some other speaker(s) or writers(s).

For web resources relevant to this book, see:
www.englishforacademicstudy.com
These weblinks will provide you with further help in inferring meaning from context and in using reporting language.

4 Society today

In this unit you will:

- make use of **prior knowledge** to help your global comprehension
- choose appropriate strategies for a specific reading purpose
- develop your note-taking skills
- understand how the title and abstract of a text can help your reading

Text	Growing grey, Text 4a (Source Book pp. 17–20)

Text 4a is an article from the *Geography Review* on issues related to an ageing population.

FOCUS TASK 👁

Your reading purpose for Tasks 1–3 is to carry out reading research on the basis of completing an essay entitled:

▶ The population of the world is ageing. What impact will this phenomenon have on society?

Imagine that in the process of your research you will read the text *Growing grey* from an article in the *Geography Review*; you will then make notes that could be used to write a short summary for use in completing the essay.

As you work through Tasks 1–3, think about how you would write this essay.

Task 1	Considering the title and the introduction

1.1 **Consider your own view of the impact of an ageing world population.**
Discuss your view with another student.

1.2 **Analyze the title.**
   a. Does the title *Growing grey* make you feel that the text may be useful to you?
   b. Discuss your views with another student.

1.3 **Read and evaluate the short opening summary to the article.**
   a. Select one sentence you think is the most relevant to your reading purpose.
   b. Explain your choice to another student.

Task 2	Considering subheadings and displayed information

Text 4a contains quite a lot of **displayed information**. Apart from the title, there are six subheadings, one photograph and three figures (maps). This information can help you predict the content of the text.

2.1 **Read the subheadings in the table. In column 2, write down what you expect to learn from each section.**

You will read the whole text in Task 3 to check whether your predictions were accurate or not. The first one has been done for you.

Subheadings	Possible contents
Who are the old?	*definition of 'old'*
Who are the very old?	
More old and very old people	
More old women	
Dependency burden	
Age-selective migration	

2.2 **Look at the photograph and three figures and discuss with other students why you think they were included in the article.**

2.3 **Study Figures 1, 2, and 3 and describe the most important detail.**

Write one sentence for each figure in the table below.

Figure 1	
Figure 2	
Figure 3	

Key reading skills: Surveying features of the text

In order to produce an appropriate summary of the text, you need to have a clear understanding of the content. Looking carefully at headings, photos and figures can help provide a way into the text and clarify the content. Once you feel you understand the content, you can move on to the next stage of the process: making notes.

Task 3 | Making notes

When preparing to make notes, you should concentrate on the main points. You only need to add examples if you feel they will be useful for your task.

3.1 **Read the introduction and the first two sections of the text.**
Do not use a dictionary at this stage, but read for general understanding. Your teacher will set a time limit.

3.2 **Write your notes.**
Write down everything you can remember in note form or as a mind map.

Key reading skills: Making notes after you read
You can often save time by making notes after you have finished reading. If you make notes as you read, it may slow down your reading and interrupt your concentration on the text.

3.3 **Repeat the procedure in Ex 3.1 and 3.2 for:**
1. Section 3
2. Sections 4 and 5
3. Section 6

Discuss your notes with other students.

3.4 **Compare your notes with the model supplied by your teacher.**
a. What do you find most interesting or effective about the notes provided by your teacher?
b. Do you think your own notes are effective?

3.5 **Reflect on your note-taking. Discuss the following with other students.**
a. What strategies did you use to carry out the task?
b. Were your strategies successful?

Key reading skills: Note-taking strategies
Reading and making notes is an essential academic skill. Making notes enables you to reflect on your understanding of the text and helps you to organize your ideas. Be prepared to try out different strategies when note-taking so that you can find what suits you best.

Note: Now you have read Text 4a, check the accuracy of your predictions in Ex 2.1.

Task 4 | Writing a summary

The final stage of the process is to organize your notes and then write your summary.

4.1 **Write your summary.**
Note: You will be able to compare your notes and summary with examples supplied by the teacher.

Text	Well connected? The biological implications of 'social networking', Text 4b (Source Book pp. 21–24)

Text 4b is an article from *The Biologist* on the effect of social networking on face-to-face contact. You will use the text to carry out further *selective* summarizing practice. Most of your note-taking will be from memory. This is to encourage you to make brief notes in your *own* words. This should help you develop a better understanding of the key points of the text, as well as encourage you to write the *summary* in your own words and avoid plagiarizing sections of the text. After making the notes, you will again be given an opportunity to check the text and revise the notes.

Task 5 Considering the title and abstract

5.1 **Analyze the title of Text 4b. Discuss questions 1–3 with other students.**
1. What do you understand by the term *social networking*?
2. How are you involved with social networking, if at all?
3. Does your idea of networking correspond with the following dictionary definition?

'the practice of meeting other people involved in the same kind of work, to share information, support each other, etc.' (Longman Dictionary of Contemporary English, 2003)

5.2 **Analyze the opening summary for Text 4b.**
Why do you think some phrases in the text have been highlighted?

> One of the most pronounced changes in the daily habits of British citizens is a reduction in the number of minutes per day that they interact with another human being. Recent history has seen people in marked retreat from one another as Britain moves from a culture of greater common experience to a society of more isolated experience. She is in good company, as Americans too step back from one another in unprecedented magnitude.

5.3 **Analyze phrases from the opening summary.**
a. Discuss the meaning of each phrase with another student, or work alone.
b. Complete the table below by explaining, in your own words, the meaning of each phrase.

Phrase	Paraphrase
pronounced changes	
reduction in the number of minutes per day	
people in marked retreat	
a culture of greater common experience	
unprecedented magnitude	

c. Answer the questions below.
1. What does *they* refer to in the second line?
2. What does *She* refer to in the final sentence?

Task 6 — Reading and making notes

6.1   **Read Section 1 of the text without stopping.**
  a.   Without looking back at the text, list the examples of how or why people in Britain and America are stepping 'back from one another in unprecedented magnitude'.
  b.   Compare your list with another student.

6.2   **Look at Figure 1 and discuss the questions below.**
  a.   What very obvious trend do you notice?
  b.   In which year did the difference between social interaction and electronic media use completely reverse?

> **Study tip**
>
> Graphs, tables and charts can summarize key information in a very economical way. Remember to look at them carefully.

6.3   **Read Section 2, *Eye and ear contact,* without stopping and then complete steps a–c without looking back at the text.**
  a.   Write down what you think the subheading *Eye and ear contact* refers to.
  b.   Write notes based on what you recall from the text.
  c.   Check the text; decide if there are any extra points you should record in your notes.

Task 7 — Making notes and drawing conclusions

The following tasks all involve reading quickly and making notes from memory.

7.1   **Read Section 3, *Morbidity.***
  When you have finished reading, write down in no more than two sentences why experts emphasize the importance of maintaining (or regaining) a culture of greater common experience.

7.2   **Read Section 4, *Marriage and cohabitation.***
  When you finish this section, complete a–c.
  a.   Make notes from memory, as in earlier tasks.
  b.   With other students, discuss what main point is being made in this section.
  c.   Write a summary of the main point in <u>one</u> sentence.

7.3   **Read Section 5, *Conclusion*, without stopping.**
  a.   Make a note of the key points from memory.
  b.   On completing your notes, decide whether you personally are concerned about any of the issues discussed in the text.
  c.   With other students, discuss any concerns you have.

8.1   **Re-read the opening summary at the beginning of Text 4b. What do you now understand by the question *Well connected?* in the title?**

8.2   **Write a text of no more than 150 words summarizing the biological implications of 'social networking'.**

When you have finished, you will be able to compare your summary with an example supplied by your teacher.

Note: Your teacher may now decide to spend more time looking at the text in order to focus on some of the vocabulary, text structure and academic style that may be useful for you to study.

Key reading skills: Writing a summary of the text

Summarizing a text involves answering the question: *What key ideas does the author want to communicate?* A summary does not have to be long and should not include too much detail.

Unit summary

Some new activities have been introduced in this fourth unit. You have also had further practice in the skills and activities introduced in earlier units.

1 **Look back over the work you have done and think about how successfully you carried out the various tasks. As you check, tick (✔) the appropriate box in the table below.**

Skills and techniques	very well	quite well	need more work	not covered
Identifying the reading purpose				
Analyzing the title and the opening summary or abstract				
Making use of subheadings or displayed information				
Critically comparing sets of notes for accuracy				
Making notes from memory and drawing conclusions				
Reflecting on note-taking strategies				
Writing a summary based on two texts				

2 **Complete the following sentences to remind yourself of the SQ3R technique.**

a. Readers can survey a text by: _____

_____

b. List possible questions readers could ask about the text *Growing Grey* by looking at the main heading and subheadings.

   What is meant by 'growing grey'? _____

_____

_____

c. By trying to find answers to questions like the ones above, the reader is reading for:

_____

d. When the reader tries to recall the text, it means: _____

e. Finally, it is important to review a text in order to ensure that: _____

For web resources relevant to this book, see:
www.englishforacademicstudy.com
These weblinks will provide you with further help in predicting the content of a text using the abstract, subheadings and displayed information.

5 Food security

In this unit you will:

- apply reading strategies: making use of assumed knowledge and displayed information
- identify key words which convey the writer's stance
- identify paragraph function and understand text organization
- use enabling skills: **annotating** the text and writing notes and summaries

FOCUS TASK

You are going to read a selection of texts in order to produce a set of notes that will help you complete the following assignment:

> The global population has increased from 2 billion to 7 billion in the past 80 years. In the next 40 years it is predicted to rise to 9 billion.
>
> What are the challenges and what measures can be most effective in feeding such a rapidly expanding population?

Text	Diet and sustainability key to feeding the world: A food security report, Text 5a (Source Book pp. 28–29)

Text 5a summarizes the key issues relating to food security that are covered in greater detail in the three other texts in the unit. These come from a review paper by UK government scientists, which maintains that good nutrition and sustainability are essential in order to ensure global food security.

Task 1   Surveying the text

It is important that students in higher education make decisions about how to make use of an academic text because of the large amount of reading required on some courses.

Study tip

Remember that surveying features of the text before going into detailed reading can save time and provide important insights into the content and value of the text. Features to look for include the title and any figures or graphs.

1.1 **Analyze the title of Text 5a by examining it in sections. Complete Column 2 with appropriate deductions. In the table below the title is divided into six separate parts.**

Note: Very useful ideas and information can be learnt from carefully analyzing the title of academic texts.

Title deconstruction	Deductions
Diet	relating to *food and nutrition* _____
sustainability	something which can be _____
key	very _____ factor(s)
feeding the world	_____
food security	having access to _____
report	a _____

1.2   Now consider what you can deduce from the photograph about the content of the text. Discuss your ideas with another student.

_____

_____

1.3   Look at the <u>references</u> at the end of the text. What useful information do these give?

_____

_____

| Task 2 | Search reading: Practising fast, accurate reading |

2.1   **Read Text 5a quickly, but carefully, to answer questions 1–12.**
Scan the text quickly to find the information you need to answer the questions. Then read the information carefully to answer accurately.

1.   What solutions for achieving food security are identified in the introductory material?

_____

2.   What two major causes of starvation on a global scale are identified?

_____

_____

3.   These two factors have resulted in there being less …

a.   _____

b.   _____

4.   The population 'explosion' is predicted to level off in …

_____

5.   Approximately how many people in total are faced with insufficient food and nutrition?

a.   1 billion   b.   2 billion   c.   3 billion

6.   What year does the Stanford University research relate to?

_____

7.   The dramatic decrease in vulture numbers in India has led to …

_____

8. What is the negative impact of developed countries importing exotic fruit?

_____

9. What could be the negative impact of poorer countries exporting exotic fruit?

_____

_____

10. Where can the impact of climate change be most effectively managed?

_____

11. In future, animals may well be the main source of …

_____

12. Which form of research is recommended for dealing with future food insecurity?

_____

| Task 3 | Identifying functions of the text |

A useful approach to understanding the organization, purpose and value of a text is to identify the functions section by section, paragraph by paragraph and if necessary, sentence by sentence. One way of doing this is by annotating the text in the margin.

Study tip

Clear annotation of text can provide useful reference for revision or further study.

3.1 **Look at the two examples of annotations for lines 5–15 of Text 5a. Then highlight the parts of the text relevant to the other two annotations.**

Annotations	Text extract (lines 5–15)
one reason further info. another reason + cause implication	Grave concerns about food security have surfaced for a number of reasons. Firstly, there has been a population explosion. According to the Royal Society, between 1930 and 2010 the world's population grew from 2 billion to 6.8 billion now, with a projected peak of 9 billion by 2050 (Black, 2010). A further major cause for concern is the impact on food production of climate change, brought about by global warming. Population growth and climate change will mean there is an increasing shortage of water and of land for food production, and therefore more competition for these resources.

3.2   **Go through the rest of the text making brief annotations in the margin. Use a pencil in case you decide to make changes.**

Identify which sections of the text have the following functions (not all of these functions might be used in this text):

- background information, e.g., giving detail of the overall situation
- general problems/implications
- exemplification, i.e., examples
- explication, i.e., further information to develop a point
- solution
- evaluation, e.g., of ideas
- viewpoints, i.e., writer's recommendations or suggestions
- conclusion

3.3   **Complete the table using the annotations you made in Ex 3.2.**

In the extra comments column you might write comments such as *relevant to the Focus task* or *check this source*.

Function	Line numbers	Extra comments
1. background information	5–15	*some reasons and implications mentioned + relevant to Focus task*
2. general problems/ implications		
3. exemplification		
4. explication		
5. solution		
6. evaluation		
7. viewpoints		
8. conclusion		

Task 4	The writer's choice of language

The writer's choice of language can also perform a particular function, for example, to indicate the seriousness or importance of the information or ideas being described. The use of adjectives or adverbs can play an important role in putting the writer's message across effectively. It can also help the reader identify examples of the writer's attitude or bias towards the topic.

4.1   **Look at lines 1–22 and identify two more examples of language that the writer uses to convey the seriousness of the topic.**

grave concerns (line 5)

4.2   **Look at lines 23–39 and list further examples of strong descriptive language the writer uses to emphasize the problems.**

brink of extinction (line 33)

_____

_____

_____

4.3   **Look at the words and phrases in the table below and find words and phrases in the text with a similar meaning.**

Complete the table with the word or phrase, its word class and the number of the line where it appears. Note that the definitions are listed in the same order as the relevant words in the text.

Study tip

Taking an interest in features of the text such as the writer's choice of language will not only help your understanding of the text, but will also help to develop your reading research skills in the long term.

Definition	Line number	Word or phrase	Word class
a. deal with (P1)			
b. appear or emerge (P2)			
c. estimated high point or maximum (P2)			
d. a large amount/many (P3)			
e. having insufficient food (P3)			
f. opposite situation (P3)			
g. total amount of greenhouse emissions (P6)			
h. very possible (P7)			
i. actions/policies (P8)			

Text	**The challenge of feeding 9 billion people, Text 5b** (Source Book pp. 30–31)

Text 5b looks in more detail at the issues we face in producing enough food to feed our growing world population.

Task 5 | Understanding the Focus task

You need to think carefully about what the task asks you to do, because it will determine what you should concentrate on in your reading. It will also determine how you read.

You are going to read three more texts and produce a set of notes that will help you complete the assignment specified in the Focus task.

5.1 **Read the first part of the Focus task. What is your reaction? Choose from 1–5.**

FOCUS TASK

> The global population has increased from 2 billion to 7 billion in the past 80 years. In the next 40 years it is predicted to rise to 9 billion.

1. I'm amazed.
2. I'm quite surprised.
3. I'm concerned.
4. I'm unconcerned.
5. I'm not surprised.

5.2 **List some possible reasons for the unprecedented phenomenon mentioned in the Focus task.**
Compare your list with those of other students.

5.3 **Now look at the second part of the Focus task and answer the two questions.**

FOCUS TASK

> What are the challenges and what measures can be most effective in feeding such a rapidly expanding population?

1. In what ways have your eating habits and those of your friends and family changed since childhood?
2. Can you explain why these changes might have occurred?

5.4 **Write answers to questions 1–5. Then discuss your answers with other students. All the questions relate to the second part of the Focus task.**

1. There are two questions. What are they?

   _____

2. Discuss these questions with other students. What do you understand by *the challenges?*

   _____

3. What do you understand by *measures?*

   _____

4. Do you need to consider all possible measures, or just the most effective ones?

   _____

5. How much background information is necessary in order to complete the task?

   _____

Task 6 — Predicting specific content in a text

You have already practised predicting content as a way of improving comprehension. Prediction can be even more effective when you focus on specific issues you expect to find in the text.

6.1 **Brainstorm ideas with other students.**
What will Text 5b identify as:
1. the main challenges involved in feeding a rapidly expanding global population?
2. the measures that need to be taken to meet these challenges?

6.2 **Read the abstract from Text 5b and compare it with what you wrote in Ex 6.1.**
The abstract briefly mentions the challenges and measures needing to be taken. Did you think of any of the same issues?

Task 7 — Identifying the main ideas

7.1 **Match the following brief summaries to the main contents of the four sections, 1–4, of the text.**
Note: There is one extra summary that is less appropriate. For this summary write N/A (not appropriate).

Summary	Section
Finding new food sources for an expanding population	
Evaluating some possible solutions	
Providing for both planetary and human needs	
Trends in food availability and prices	
Identifying the future global challenges	

Discuss your answers with another student.

Task 8 — Addressing the Focus task

8.1 **Re-read the text and write notes relating to the challenges the Focus task mentions and necessary measures that need to be taken.**
a. Read the text once and write brief notes relevant to the assignment.
b. Discuss your notes with another student and amend them if necessary.
c. Refer back to the text and add any further notes if appropriate.
d. Use your notes to help you complete the table on the next page.

Challenges	Measures

Key reading skills: Developing your notes

Well-written notes will provide you with an effective tool for revision and writing research. You should therefore practise developing your own style of note-taking – one that works for you. Bear in mind that your notes will always be more effective if you have a clear idea of what information you wish to extract from the text before you begin reading.

Task 9	Logic and language

A well-written paragraph should be both coherent and cohesive. The task below will provide further practice in organizing a paragraph in such a way. Remember to pay attention to cohesive markers, such as linking words and expressions, and any pronoun referencing or other words/phrases that link back to previous ideas.

Study tip

Recognizing coherence and cohesion in a text will benefit your writing as well as your understanding of the text.

9.1 **Reorganize the paragraph in the table below in a logical order. Number the sentences 1–5.**

Sentences	Number
Particular emphasis should be given to sustainability.	
Recent studies suggest that the world will need 70 to 100% more food by 2050.	
Only when this has been fully established might a global catastrophe be avoided.	
Major strategies for contributing to the challenge of feeding 9 billion people, including the most disadvantaged, therefore need to be explored.	
At the same time, the combined role of the natural and social sciences in analyzing and addressing the challenge of feeding the poorest must be prioritized.	

Key reading skills: Coherence and cohesion

A well-written text should be both coherent and cohesive. The coherence comes from the logical ordering of the text content and the cohesion comes from the appropriate use of linguistic features such as cohesive markers, e.g., *however*, *subsequently*, *in this respect*, *these*, etc.

Task 10 — Working out meaning from context

10.1 **Complete the table below with words or phrases of the same or similar meaning (i.e., *synonyms*) from Text 5b, Sections 1–3. Write the word class and the line number where it appears in the text.**

Note: The words in column 1 are listed in the same order as the relevant synonyms in the text.

Synonym	Word or phrase	Word class	Line number
significant (S1)			
stop increasing (S1)			
approximately (S1)			
competition (S1)			
concerning (S1)			
having greater wealth (S2)			
far-reaching/very significant (S2)			
interspersed (S3)			
sudden sharp rises (S3)			
decreased (S3)			
unstable (S3)			
encourage (S3)			

Key reading skills: Selecting useful vocabulary

The words in Ex 10.1 have been selected because they could be very useful for you to know and to be able to use during your future academic studies. Always think carefully about which words are the most useful to learn and use. Try to work out the meaning of such words (if you do not already know them) from the context and then record them in your vocabulary notebook.

| Text | Closing the yield gap, Text 5c (Source Book pp. 32–34) |

One major decision you need to make when reading an academic text is to decide which parts of the text are the most relevant to your reading needs. This will save you time and allow you to make the best use of the most relevant material.

Text 5c consists of ten paragraphs, including the introductory material. These paragraphs have various different purposes or functions, such as: describing problems, giving a definition, outlining the situation, analysis and discussion and looking at solutions.

| Task 11 | **Identifying the function of paragraphs** |

11.1 **Read the list of functions 1–5. Discuss with another student which paragraphs they might refer to in the text.**

1. Discussion and analysis
2. Problems
3. Conclusion
4. Evaluation
5. Solutions

11.2 **Read Text 5c as quickly as possible and complete the table with the function (or functions) that best applies to each paragraph.**

Paragraph	Main function or functions	Most useful paragraphs
1		
2		
3		
4		
5		
6	discussion and analysis (and evaluation)	
7		
8		
9		
10		

11.3 **Tick (✔) the relevant paragraphs in the table above to indicate which are most useful in helping you produce further notes relevant to the Focus task.**

12.1 **Study the following example notes developed from paragraphs 1–5 of the text.**
  a. Decide whether any further notes or annotations could be added.
  b. Briefly summarize the notes in the summary section at the bottom of the table.

BIBLIOGRAPHICAL DETAILS

Godfray, H. C. J., Beddington, J. R., Crute, I. R., Haddad, L., Lawrence, D., Muir, J. F., et al. (2010). The challenge of feeding 9 billion people. Science. 327(5967), 812–818.

ANNOTATIONS	NOTES
definition 'yield gap' useful (see first para.)	(from 'Closing the yield gap' lines 3–7)
	Challenges:
	Level of food production varies greatly depending on region, e.g., Africa had far lower production increases than China/Latin America – need to close yield gap
Example needed?	Low yields due to technical constraints + econ. reasons driven by market forces
	Lack of tech. knowledge + skills
Does this include all forms of food production?	Limited finances
	Lack of storage space
	Lack of investment by farmers – poor returns + 'poverty trap'
Solutions	Balance needed between investing in overall growth and focusing on agricultural growth
	Focusing on overall growth leading to buying from more developed system may be best choice
	Need to have developed infrastructure before yield gap can be addressed
More problems	Factors such as poor transport system, limited market infrastructure = higher prices of inputs

SUMMARY

The Cornell note-taking system

The Cornell note-taking system was developed by Walter Pauk, emeritus professor of education at Cornell University in the United States. It is the page layout of Cornell notes that makes this system different from other ways of note-taking. A single sheet of paper is divided into a left- and a right-hand column, with a row at the bottom and a row at the top. The four resulting sections each have a specific purpose.

The row at the top should include all the bibliographical details, including the name(s) of the author(s), the title of the original article, the source, the date of publication, the volume number if the text comes from a journal, and the page numbers. A book should also have the name of the publisher and the place (city or town) of publication.

The space in the right-hand column is the *note-taking* area. Here there is sufficient room to write down ideas, impressions and notes that are made from a text or during a lecture. It is usually when these notes have been completed that the left column and bottom area are used, although some annotating may go on during the note-taking stage.

The left column is then used to *annotate* the notes with comments, questions, references, reminders, extra ideas or interpretations. This annotation process is a crucial element in note-taking. It provides the opportunity to consider the notes, digest and fully understand them. It may lead the note-taker to add ideas or expand the information.

The bottom area leaves space for the main notes on each page to be summarized. The summary provides a concise review of the key facts that have been identified and can be used for reference later.

12.2 **Using the Cornell system, continue making notes, annotations and summaries for the remaining relevant parts of the text and complete the table below.**

ANNOTATIONS	NOTES

SUMMARY

12.3　**Look at the following questions and underline the words or phrases in Text 5c that answer them.**

Note: In Unit 1, you read about and practised the SQ3R approach to reading a text. In this exercise, the focus is on the second of the five phases involved in this method – asking questions about the text.

1. What is a *yield gap*?
2. What would be the two most significant results if the yield gap was reduced?
3. Which area of the world has not increased its food production level?
4. What two key factors prevent some poorer farmers from achieving high yields?
5. What impact can a limited transport and market infrastructure have?
6. What positive result can the globalization of the food system have?
7. What does the concept of *sustainability* suggest?
8. What system might be established to improve the income of the rural poor in the more underdeveloped regions?
9. Why is it important for the land rights of the very poor to be protected?
10. What can social protection programmes do to safeguard the ability of the rural poor to be adequately fed?

12.4　**Check whether the notes in your Cornell note-taking grid include answers to the questions in Ex 12.3.**
a. Add any extra notes as necessary.
b. Transform any other notes you have made into appropriate note form if you consider them relevant to the focus question.

Key reading skills: Checking your notes
Asking questions about the text not only helps you gain a better understanding of the text, it also allows you to check how effective your notes are.

Text	Dealing with the situation, Text 5d (Source Book pp. 35–39)

Text 5d addresses the problem of how to feed a rapidly expanding population and looks at solutions.

Task 13	Predicting the content of the text

Before you read, you will make some predictions about what sort of ideas the text contains.

13.1　**Read the question and write at least four possible solutions to the problem.**
What strategies and actions do you think might most effectively solve the huge problem of feeding the rapidly expanding global population?

_____

_____

_____

_____

13.2 **Compare and discuss your predictions with other students.**

Try to agree on one that you all feel would be the most effective.

Note: Later, one of your main reading objectives will be to check whether your predictions and those of other students are mentioned in the text, and which solutions the researchers emphasize as being the most effective.

Task 14	**Identifying the main ideas**

14.1 **Read section headings 1–5 and match them to the sections in Text 5d.**

There are four main sections in the text – as well as the conclusion – so you will not need one of the headings.

Headings	Sections
Reducing waste	
Improving infrastructures	
Expanding aquaculture	
Increasing production limits	
Changing diets	

14.2 **Analyze your reading strategy.**

Discuss with another student the strategies you used to identify the headings and how effective they were.

Task 15	**Identifying and dealing with assumed knowledge**

Academic texts often contain certain *assumed knowledge*. This is knowledge that the writer assumes the reader already has, and which does not therefore need explanation, definition or support with a reference. For example, in Section 1 of Text 5d, the writer assumes the reader is already familiar with the idea of *Green Revolution*.

15.1 **Find more examples of assumed knowledge in Section 1.**

15.2 **Match the phrases you found in Ex 15.1 with definitions 1–5.**

1. They involve a wide variety of laboratory methods, including the modification of embryos, sex selection and genetic engineering. = _____

2. Relating to two or more genes. As opposed to *monogenic*. Eye colour is an example. = _____

3. A field of applied biology that involves the use of living organisms and bioprocesses in engineering, technology, medicine and other fields. = _____

4. A plant has this if it can survive a dry spell of more than two or three months without supplemental watering. = _____

5. This can be defined as the negative impact of non-living factors on the living organisms in a specific environment; for example, caused by cold, salt, drought or some forms of metal in the vicinity. = _____

| Task 16 | **Making use of displayed information** |

You have practised surveying the text and have looked at a variety of displayed information in earlier units and tasks. Displayed information such as artwork, tables of data, bar, pie and flow charts, maps, photographs and timelines are often referred to as graphics.

16.1 **Look at Figure 4 in the text. What do you understand by the terms listed?**

1. On-farm: _____

2. Transport and processing: _____

3. Retail: _____

4. Food service: _____

5. Home and municipal: _____

16.2 **Now answer the questions below relating to Figure 4.**

1. What is being described and in which specific areas?

_____

2. Suggest why 'retail, food service, home and municipal' have been combined for developing countries.

_____

3. Which area has the greatest amount of retail wastage?

_____

4. Which area has the most 'on-farm' wastage?

_____

5. Which has the least?

_____

6. Approximately what percentage of wastage in the UK occurs in the retail trade?

_____

16.3 **Summarize the most significant data that Figure 4 displays. Write no more than two sentences.**

_____

_____

_____

16.4 **Find an example in the text that supports your summary.**

_____

_____

Key reading skills: Making use of displayed information

Displayed information has a significant purpose as well as decorating or breaking up a text, and should not be neglected when you are reading. For example, when you are surveying texts, graphics can quickly give you an understanding of the overall contents as they summarize or exemplify what is being described. You need to develop your ability to 'interpret' the graphical information being displayed and to appreciate the most significant aspects.

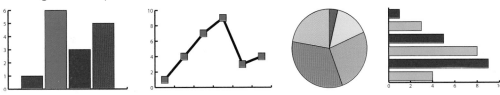

Task 17 | Producing notes

17.1 **Complete the following notes on food wastage taken from Section 2, using no more than five extra words per line to complete the notes.**

You will have to think carefully about what to take from the text and 'transform' the wording of some of the text to complete the task.

In the developing world, food wastage is mainly due to:

■ absence of _____

■ lack of _____

■ insufficient _____

■ the immediate _____

In the developed world, food wastage is mainly due to:

■ less incentive to _____

■ throwing away _____

■ promotion of _____

■ too much dependency on _____

■ misuse of _____

Unit summary

Some new activities have been introduced in the fifth unit. You have also had further practice in some activities that were introduced in the earlier units. The activities are listed below.

1 **Look back over the work you have done and think about how successfully you carried out the various tasks. As you check, tick (✔) the appropriate box in the table below.**

Skills and techniques	very well	quite well	need more work	not covered
Search reading				
Surveying texts				
Identifying text function				
Appreciating the writer's use of language				
Meeting the reading purpose				
Predicting content				
Identifying main ideas				
Understanding coherence and cohesion				
Identifying the function of paragraphs				
Annotating the text using the Cornell system				
Using the SQ3R approach to question the text				
Identifying and dealing with assumed knowledge				
Making use of displayed information/graphics				
Writing effective notes				

2 **Complete the statements by using appropriate phrases from the word box.**
Note: One of the phrases is not used.

> survey, question, read, recall, review
> work out the meaning from context   typical functions of paragraphs
> the use of linking words   the Cornell system   their reading purpose
> graphics and other displayed information are   analyzing the title

a. Heavy reading loads can be reduced if students think about _____

_____

b. Readers can decide on the usefulness of a text by first _____

c. Detailing background information, exemplifying and explicating are amongst the _____

d. An unfamiliar word is often remembered and understood more successfully if a reader tries to _____

e. _____ is a method of making notes, noting biographical details and summarizing the content of texts.

f. The formula *SQ3R* stands for _____

g. _____ useful because they provide the reader with a brief summary of the content of texts.

3 **Study the following sentences from a section of Text 5c, *Closing the yield gap*. Renumber them in what you consider is the most coherent way.**

a. However, the environmental costs of food production might increase with globalization, for example, because of increased greenhouse gas emissions associated with increased production and food transport (Pretty et al., 2005). ☐

b. Conversely, a highly connected food system may lead to the more widespread propagation of economic concerns, as in the recent banking crisis, thus affecting more people. ☐

c. Because the expansion of food production and the growth of population both occur at different rates in different geographic regions, global trade is necessary to balance supply and demand across regions. ☐

d. An unfettered market can also penalize particular communities and sectors – especially the poorest, who have the least influence on how global markets are structured and regulated. Expanded trade can provide insurance against regional shocks affecting production, such as conflict, epidemics, droughts, or floods – shocks that are likely to increase in frequency as climate change occurs. ☐

Check your order by looking at page 33 in the Source Book, lines 102–125.

4 **Indicate the linking devices used to make the text more cohesive by annotating the text appropriately.**

For web resources relevant to this book, see:
www.englishforacademicstudy.com
These weblinks will provide you with further help with identifying paragraph functions and with note-taking systems, particularly the Cornell note-taking system.

6 Human resource management

In this unit you will:

- activate schemata and focus on key definitions
- identify key points and supporting ideas
- improve your note-taking and summarizing skills
- practise fast, accurate reading for detail

In this unit you are going to study human resource management, or HRM. In particular, the texts will be about international human resource management (IHRM). This topic has been selected because the need to consider 'human' resources and how to manage them can be applied to various fields of academic study.

You will do a number of tasks before reading the text in order to access your own knowledge and ideas about the topics. This process is known as *activating schemata* and is a key process in improving reading skills.

| **Text** | Background and origins of people management, Text 6a
(Source Book pp. 40–42) |

Task 1   Defining the topic

1.1 **Consider the following questions and then discuss them with another student.**
   1. What is a resource?
   2. Can a resource be human? Why/why not?

1.2 **Write your own definition of a resource below.**

_____

1.3 **Write two sentences describing how a human resource can be best managed.**
   Think about the mechanism for management and ways to get the best out of the workforce.

_____

_____

_____

1.4 **Apart from Management (including International Management) what other academic disciplines do you think might include an element of human resource management?**

Task 2	**Expanding definitions**

2.1   **Study the following definitions of HRM and complete the gaps with words from the box.**

managers	~~recruitment~~	performs	employee (x2)	development
impede	asking	treatment	serve	allocating
opportunities	systems	includes	organizational	

1. Human Resource Management (HRM) is the function within an organization that focuses on _recruitment_ of, management of, and providing direction for the people who work in the organization. Human Resource Management can also be performed by line _____.

2. Human Resource Management is the _____ function that deals with issues related to people, such as compensation, hiring, performance management, organization _____, safety, wellness, benefits, _____ motivation, communication, administration, and training.[1]

3. Managing human resources refers to the functions that a manager _____ relative to the organization's employees. Managing human resources _____, but is not limited to:

    ■ planning and _____ resources

    ■ providing direction, vision and goals

    ■ supplying or _____ for the metrics that tell people how successfully they are performing

    ■ offering _____ for both formal and informal development

    ■ setting an example in work ethics, _____ of people, and empowerment worthy of being emulated by others

    ■ leading organization efforts to listen to and _____ customers

    ■ managing the performance management _____

    ■ challenging the _____ to maintain momentum

    ■ removing obstacles that _____ the employee's progress

    [1] **Source:** Heathfield, S. M. (2011). What is human resource management? *About.com*. Retrieved July 9, 2011, from http://humanresources.about.com/od/glossaryh/f/hr_management.htm

2.2 **Identify and highlight the key words in the definitions below.**

You will use these key words later to write a paragraph comparing the different definitions. The first one has been done as an example.

Definitions of human resource management on the Internet

1. Human resource management (HRM) is the strategic and coherent approach to the management of an organization's most valued assets – the people working there who individually and collectively contribute to the achievement of the objectives of the business. en.wikipedia.org/wiki/Human_resource_management

2. All methods and functions concerning the mobilization and development of personnel as human resources, with the objective of efficiency and greater productivity in a company, government administration, or other organization. en.wiktionary.org/wiki/Human_Resource_Management

3. Human resource management (HRM) is the understanding and application of the policy and procedures that directly affect the people working within the project team and working group. These policies include recruitment, retention, reward, personal development, training and career development. www.apm.org.uk/Definitions.asp

4. Human resource management is the effective use of human resources in order to enhance organizational performance. wps.prenhall.com/wps/media/objects/213/218150/glossary.html

5. The management of the workforce of a business to ensure sufficient staff levels with the right skills, properly rewarded and motivated. www.business2000.ie/resources/Glossary_H.html

6. Staffing function of the organization. It includes the activities of human resources planning, recruitment, selection, orientation, training, performance appraisal, compensation, and safety. www.crfonline.org/orc/glossary/h.html

7. Human Resource Management ('HRM') is a way of management that links people-related activities to the strategy of a business or organization. HRM is often referred to as 'strategic HRM'. It has several goals:
   - To meet the needs of the business and management (rather than just serve the interests of employees)
   - To link human resource strategies/policies to the business goals and objectives
   - To find ways for human resources to 'add value' to a business
   - To help a business gain the commitment of employees to its values, goals and objectives

   http://tutor2u.net/business/people/hrm_introduction.htm

> **Study tip**
>
> When you are researching an essay, it is important to look critically at various definitions of key terms.

Task 3	**Completing notes: Building background information**

According to Heathfield (2011), human resource management (HRM) is:

> … the function within an organization that focuses on recruitment of, management of, and providing direction for the people who work in the organization. Human Resource Management can also be performed by line managers. Human Resource Management is the organizational function that deals with issues related to people, such as compensation, hiring, performance management, organization development, safety, wellness, benefits, employee motivation, communication, administration, and training.

All elements of business strategy have implications for human resources, as illustrated in the table in Ex 3.1. The challenge for management is to identify and respond to these HR changes.

An important **reading strategy** is to follow the links between ideas in a text. The following task will help you link issues and implications.

3.1   **Read the five examples of business strategy issues in column 1 of the table and the implications in column 2. Add one further implication for each of the five examples, using questions 1–5 below.**

Examples of key strategy issues	Possible human resource implications
1. What markets should the business compete in?	▪ _____ ▪ What expertise is required in these markets?
2. Where should the business be located to compete optimally?	▪ Where are the people most needed? ▪ _____
3. How can we achieve improvements in our unit production costs to remain competitive?	▪ How productive is the current workforce? ▪ _____ ▪ What investment, (e.g., training, recruitment and equipment) is required to achieve the desired improvement in productivity?
4. How can the business effect cultural change?	▪ _____ ▪ How can the prevailing culture be influenced to help implement a change programme?
5. How can the business respond to rapid technological change in its markets?	▪ What technological skills does the business currently possess? ▪ What additional skills are needed to respond to technological change? ▪ _____

1.   What are their current working practices and future needs?

2.   What markets do the competitors operate in?

3.   Does existing management have the right experience to manage change?

4.   How many are needed?

5.   Can these skills be acquired through training or recruitment?

Source: Adapted from tutor2u. (2011). *Human resources management: Introduction.* Retrieved October 27, 2011, from http://www.tutor2u.net/business/people/hrm_introduction.htm

Task 4	Vocabulary extension

4.1 Read the following two definitions of the term *resource*. Which do you think is the best definition in relation to the text you are going to read, *Background and origins of people management*?

> The resources of an organization or person are the materials, money, and other things that they have and can use in order to function properly.
> Collins Cobuild Dictionary for Advanced Learners

> Something such as money, workers, or equipment that can be used to help an institution or business.
> The Macmillan English Dictionary for Advanced Learners

4.2 Compare these definitions to the ones you gave in Ex 1.2. How similar are they?

4.3 Read the following explanation. Then complete the gaps in the sentences below with forms of the word *resource*, used either as a noun or as a verb.

In the phrase *human resource management*, the word *resource* is a noun. This word can also be a verb, e.g. *The university's latest building project was resourced through funds donated by local businesses.*

1. It was decided to _____ the administration department by employing four new secretarial staff.

2. One of the most important _____ Sierra Leone has is its mineral wealth.

3. The new library was partially _____ with books donated by charitable organizations.

4. Many academic institutions _____ their lecture theatres with technologically advanced equipment since the beginning of the decade.

5. If we _____ the company more efficiently we would more easily overcome the problems caused by the current economic climate.

6. The company has _____, so now all that is needed is a suitable location to build its new showroom.

4.4 One way of activating a word and being able to remember it for future use is to produce sentences *of your own*. Write sentences to help activate the word *resource* both as a noun and a verb.

Use the sentences from Ex 4.3 as a model.

_____

_____

_____

_____

4.5 **Now write a paragraph explaining what you understand by *HRM*. Use the definitions and the key vocabulary that you identified in the previous tasks.**

Task 5	Developing ideas about the topic

Before reading a text, it is useful to consider other information and the knowledge you already have about the topic so you can bring this knowledge to the text.

5.1 **Read the following facts about the building of the Great Wall of China and answer the questions.**

> The Great Wall of China took over a thousand years to build, it was over 1,500 miles in length and more than one million people were involved in its construction.

1. How do you think the chief builders managed this project? Discuss with another student and then write down at least one idea below.

     _____

     _____

2. How many different categories of worker, e.g., farmers, do you think existed in ancient times? Make a short list and then discuss with other students. Add to your list after discussion, if appropriate.

     _____

     _____

3. Can you think of any other great projects that were carried out before the development of modern industrial techniques? Make a short list.

     _____

     _____

     _____

     _____

Key reading skills: Activating schemata
Effective readers unconsciously call to mind a schema (previous knowledge or experience) of the topic they are reading about. This contributes to their understanding of the way the text is organized and helps understanding of key concepts and vocabulary.

6.1 **Read section headings 1–7 and match them to the sections 1–6 in Text 6a.**

    a. Read the summary headings and underline the most important word(s) in each heading. If necessary, your teacher will explain the meaning of some of the language used in the headings.

    b. Read the text and identify the appropriate section, 1–6. You will not use one of the headings.

Summary headings	Sections
1. The development of HRM systems	
2. A hierarchical system of management	
3. Applying a scientific method of managing the workforce	
4. How ancient man organized tasks	
5. Books about human resource management	
6. The control of huge workforces in the past	
7. Managing large workforces in the Industrial Age	

Key reading skills: Guessing words in context

If you cannot immediately work out the meaning of unknown words from the context, continue reading rather than immediately consulting a dictionary. The wider context may be enough to help your understanding.

Try to apply the same strategy with any content you don't understand while you are reading. This will help you learn to 'tolerate ambiguity', which is a characteristic of good language learners.

6.2 **Guess the meaning of the phrase 'tolerate ambiguity'.**

Ambiguous means unclear. *Tolerate* means to put up with something.
What does to 'tolerate ambiguity' mean?

Task 7   Making use of the text

This task will give you a practical demonstration of the division of labour, a concept dealt with in the opening paragraph of Text 6a. You will first read the introduction and define the concept; then in Ex 6.2 you will experience the process for yourselves.

7.1 **Read Section 1 of Text 6a and consider what is meant by 'the division of labour'. Then complete the sentence below.**

The division of labour means _____

_____

_____

7.2 **Simulate the preparation for a group presentation.**
Imagine that your Human Geography class has been divided into groups of four students to carry out the following group presentation. **Note:** You do <u>not</u> have to give the presentation itself.

> Give a 30-minute presentation on the advantages and disadvantages of having a ban on all private transport during the working week.

This assignment forms a significant part of your overall assessment of a module on town planning, so you will need to work well as a team. Imagine the following scenario:

- You have three hours to create and give the presentation.
- You must use at least four sources of information (only two online sources are allowed).
- You should produce a handout based on your presentation with copies of your presentation slides for all 60 other students in the class.
- You need to rehearse your presentation and edit all the slides.
- All group members must be able to answer questions at the end of the presentation.

Carry out the task as follows:
a. Work in groups of four.
b. Consider your individual strengths.
c. Based on your conclusions, draw up a plan of action showing how the work will be carried out.
d. Produce a representation of your division of labour for display to other students; be prepared to justify your actions.

Task 8	Identifying and summarizing key points

This task will help you extract key points from the text to help you complete the Focus task.

FOCUS TASK

You are going to make a series of notes in order to complete the following task:

> Task management has gone through various stages of development. Briefly describe this development as outlined in the text.

8.1 Use information from Section 1 of Text 6a to complete the following list. Write single words or short phrases.

Factors that have determined allocation of roles and responsibilities
1. Skill
2.
3.
4. Social group
5.
6.
7. Best people for job
8.
9. Specialist knowledge
10.

8.2 Use information from Section 2 to complete the list of examples from the ancient world (where huge groups of people had to be organized).

Situations that needed organization in the ancient world
1. Building the pyramids
2.
3.
4.
5.

8.3 Use information from Section 3 to complete the table. Use no more than five words in each cell.

Individual	System of management
Niccolò Machiavelli	
	Division of labour
George Cadbury	

8.4   **Use information from Sections 4, 5 and 6 to complete the following flow charts.**

Flow chart illustrating the McCallum system of management

Manageable divisions _____   ▼

_____   ▼

_____   ▼

_____   ▼

Flow chart showing the development of scientific management

_____   ▼

_____   ▼

_____   ▼

_____   ▼

_____   ▼

8.5   **Using the information you recorded in Ex 8.1–8.4, write a summary as outlined in the Focus task. Your summary should not be longer than 150 words.**

Task 9	Main points and supporting ideas

When reading an academic text, it is important to consider the function of sentences. Understanding how sentences working in unison help the reader differentiate the main idea from the supporting ideas.

The exercises below summarize some of the functions that sentences may perform within a paragraph.

9.1   **Read the list and complete the gaps in each sentence with words from the box.**
Note: You will not use all of the words.

link   secondary   idea   key   develop   write   explain

Sentences may:

1.   introduce a new _____ which is the focus of the paragraph.

2.   provide a _____ between paragraphs.

3.   _____ an idea which has already been introduced in the 'focus' sentence.

4.   summarize the _____ point or points.

5.   introduce a _____ point.

9.2 **Look at the following paragraphs from the text.**
  a. Identify the main point and <u>underline</u> or highlight it.
  b. In the column next to the paragraph, briefly summarize the main point in your own words.
  c. Study the development of each supporting point in other sentences.

  Note: The main point may not always be the first sentence in a paragraph. Summarizing the main point can help you to predict the functions of the **supporting sentences**.

Paragraph	Notes
1. In the ancient world, social customs determined separate roles and tasks for males and females. 2. Traditional self-sufficient communities dependent on agriculture or fishing rarely had more than 20–30 categories of labour, in contrast to modern industrial states that have thousands of different job types. 3. Some functions, such as religious and political leadership or medicine, were restricted to individuals with inherited or specialist knowledge. 4. As civilization and technology evolved, however, specialization led to a proliferation of different forms of work. 5. In this way, hunters, farmers and fishermen were joined by skilled craftworkers using metal, pottery or wood.	In the past, men and woman customarily had different jobs to do.

9.3 **Study the table, which describes the function of the supporting points from sentences 2–5 in Ex 9.2.**

Sentence	Function
2	contrasts past with present situation
3	example of past situation
4	example of developing situation
5	summarizes development of situation

9.4 **Repeat the procedure in Ex 9.2–9.3 with Section 6 from Text 6a.**

Paragraph	Notes
1. Meanwhile, a distinctive form of scientific management was taken up in the new high-volume production industries. **2.** This became known as 'Fordism' after the mass-production methods used by Henry Ford for automobile manufacturing. **3.** Scientific management had first been developed by F. W. Taylor in *Shop Management*, outlining a system of extracting maximum output from workers. **4.** Jelink (quoted in Mintzberg, 1994: 21) considers that Taylor 'for the first time made possible the large-scale coordination, planning and policy-level thinking, above and beyond the details of the task itself'. **5.** This produced a new division of labour, splitting tasks and their coordination into different roles. **6.** So management had become 'abstracted' from everyday activities, allowing it to 'concentrate on exceptions'.	

Sentence	Function
2	
3	
4	
5	
6	

Text	International human resource management, Text 6b (Source Book pp. 43–44)

Text 6b is an extract from a book on human resource management and will provide some useful information on international aspects of the discipline.

Task 10 Practising fast, accurate reading

10.1 **When your teacher tells you to, read through Text 6b without stopping. Read as quickly as you can.**

Time yourself while you are reading (divide the time it took by the number of words). Note the time before you begin reading and note it again when you have finished. There are 737 words in the text.

10.2 **Write down as much as you can remember about the text, in note form.**

Compare your notes with another student. Then review the text and add to your notes.

10.3 **Produce a mind map or flow chart to demonstrate your understanding of the text.**

Task 11 Using research as evidence

Text 6b refers extensively to academic studies carried out in the field.

Key reading skills: Referring to academic research
Identifying references to academic research in a text is one way of judging its credibility as well as supporting the writer's argument.

11.1 **Re-read Text 6b and match statements 1–7 below with the experts mentioned in the text. Write the name of the academic cited next to each point.**

Note: The statements are paraphrases of information in the text.

Descriptions	Academic
1. IHRM has mainly focused on personnel working permanently or temporarily overseas.	
2. An interest in the 'international' aspect of HRM started to develop about 25 years ago.	
3. IHRM needs to consider the workforce, the infrastructure of the business, and the development of an appropriate cultural understanding of internationalization.	
4. It is crucial that a company looks after its resources and funding so that the business is effectively managed worldwide.	
5. The cultural challenge of managing a multinational company is a crucial element in effective IHRM.	
6. Research in international human resource management has been extremely limited.	
7. Comparing how companies are managed in terms of human resources is not the same as IHRM.	

Task 12 | Identifying the writer's purpose

12.1 **The writer uses a range of expert opinions to support his writing purpose. What do you consider is the writer's main purpose?**
Choose one of the following options.
1. to outline recent developments in IHRM
2. to compare opinions about what IHRM is
3. to illustrate the difference between HRM and IHRM
4. to describe the history of IHRM

12.2 **Explain your choice.**

_____

_____

_____

_____

_____

Task 13 | Preparing notes

FOCUS TASK 👁

Your aim in reading this text is to prepare a set of notes to support a discussion on the following topic:

> ▶ Human resource management is the most crucial factor in creating a thriving enterprise at both national and international level.

13.1 With reference to both texts in this unit, find any relevant details and then prepare a set of notes or produce a mind map.

Unit summary

Some new activities have been introduced in this unit. You have also had further practice in some activities that were introduced in earlier units. The activities are listed below.

1 **Look back over the work you have done and think about how successfully you carried out the various tasks. As you check, tick (✔) the appropriate box in the table below.**

Skills and techniques	very well	quite well	need more work	not covered
Defining the topic				
Thinking about and expanding definitions				
Developing ideas about a topic/completing notes				
Identifying and summarizing relevant information				
Differentiating between main and supporting ideas in a text				
Scanning texts for specific details				
Practising fast, accurate reading using research as evidence				
Identifying the writer's purpose				

2 **Study the examples below of words that function as both nouns and verbs.**

There are many words in the English language that function as nouns or verbs, depending on the context.

Example:
1. A <u>reward</u> for Saif's hard work was to see his article in print.
2. If you <u>reward</u> students for their work, they will feel a sense of motivation.

In some cases, the syllable stress will change depending on whether the function of the word is a verb or a noun.

Use a dictionary to check the words in the box. Notice how the stress shifts between the noun and the verb and how the dictionary indicates this shift of stress.

Try to construct simple sentences using the words listed below, first as nouns and then as verbs. This will help you commit them to your active lexicon.

record	increase	finance	survey	research

Do further work online.
Go to the following website and try out the activities:
http://www.english-online.org.uk/games/verbnounboth.htm

For web resources relevant to this book, see:
www.englishforacademicstudy.com
These weblinks will provide you with further help in developing strategies to use your background knowledge and ideas to improve reading skills, as well as further help on writing summaries.

7 Sustainable fashion

In this unit you will:

- apply reading strategies: monitor your understanding of the text while you are reading; focus more closely on your reading purpose
- use research skills: compare your views (as a reader) with those of the writer
- identify the writer's purpose and the function of different parts of the text
- analyze the titles, subtitles and the other displayed information

FOCUS TASK

You are going to read three texts about sustainable fashion in order to take and annotate notes that will help you complete the following assignment.

> The fashion industry poses a serious threat to the environment. A higher level of sustainability in materials production is the key solution. Discuss.

It is generally accepted that sustainable design is aimed at providing products which are made only of renewable resources. As such, the products should have minimal impact on the environment during any stage of their design, creation, processing, use or final disposal. A fundamental principle in sustainable design is that it should appeal to the consumer physically, emotionally and economically – in other words, products must look good, make the consumer feel good about using them and, if possible, be generally affordable.

Text	Material diversity, Text 7a (Source Book pp. 45–48)

Task 1	Before you read

1.1 Discuss the concepts of *sustainability* and *fashion* with other students.

  a. Discuss and then write down five words (or ideas/concepts):
  - relevant to fashion
  - relevant to sustainability
  b. Think about why there is tension between the concepts of sustainability and fashion.

1.2 Before reading Text 7a, think about the title *Material diversity*.

  a. What do you understand by the word *diversity*?
  b. What do you think *material diversity* is, and why might it be important?

Task 2	**Surveying the text**

Surveying the text before you read can help you to decide on the usefulness of the text. It can also help you to read more effectively. Text 7a contains several examples of displayed information.

2.1 **Survey the text and note the examples of displayed information. What is the purpose of the first example? Discuss your ideas with another student.**

2.2 **Study Tables 1 and 2.**
1. What type of information do they each contain?
2. What can you infer from the information in Table 1?

Discuss your ideas with another student.

Task 3	**Identifying the main ideas**

3.1 **Read the text and, as you read*, match the headings a–h below with Sections 1–8 of Text 7a.**

*You may find it useful first to read through the headings and identify what you think are key words. You can then look for synonyms in each paragraph. It is also very useful to identify the **paragraph leader** in each paragraph and to look at the concluding sentence.

Headings		Section
a.	How different methods of fibre production can impact on sustainability	
b.	The pros and cons of both synthetic and natural fibre production	
c.	The important link between diversification and greater sustainability	
d.	The raw material sources of natural and manufactured fibres	
e.	The link between research and the development of a sustainable fashion industry	
f.	Scientific, social and ethical reasons for changing attitudes about fibre production	
g.	The accuracy of research findings relating to the use of appropriate fibres for sustainable fashion	
h.	A review of global demand for natural and manufactured fibres	

Task 4	Identifying functions of the text

This task focuses on the functions of different parts of the text. It will help you to understand how a text is logically constructed and how the writer develops his or her thesis.

The information in Section 1 of Text 7a is organized in a particular way, where parts of the text serve different functions.

4.1   **Before you read, look at the range of functions in the table below and match each one with a description.**

Functions	Descriptions	Function number
1. evaluation	a. the outcomes, consequences or effects of doing something or of something happening	
2. problem(s)	b. when a new point is introduced or about to be introduced; usually occurs at the beginning or the end of a paragraph or section of text	
3. background	c. the answer to a problem, or the process of arriving at an answer	
4. summing up	d. matters that involve difficulties and need solutions	
5. cause	e. judgement or analysis of, e.g., solutions to certain problems	
6. transition	f. concluding remarks which encapsulate ideas previously presented; often found at the end of a section of text, but not always	
7. solution	g. a strong statement that presents the writer's main argument or claim to the reader	
8. result(s)	h. the reason for something happening, that has results or consequences	
9. thesis statement	i. information that sets the scene and/or looks at an existing situation; usually at the beginning of a section or text, but not always	3

4.2 **Complete the annotation of Section 1, reproduced below. This will show how you can annotate the text by highlighting relevant parts according to their functions.**

a. Re-read the text, paying close attention to the two annotations already made.

b. Locate, highlight and annotate other parts of the text that demonstrate the remaining functions from the table in Ex. 4.1.

c. Compare your annotations with another student's. Then compare them with a model your teacher will provide.

Bibliographical details	
Annotations	**Text**
Background	Diversity of materials and ideas is hard to find in the modern fashion and textile industry. It is dominated by a large number of similar, ready-made products in a limited range of fibre types. Indeed, cotton and polyester together account for over 80 per cent of the global market in textiles (Simpson, 2006). The result of producing large volumes of limited fibres is to concentrate impacts in specific agricultural or manufacturing sectors, to increase ecological risk, to make the sector less resilient to changing global conditions in both business and the environment and to reduce customer choice. Yet a sustainability-driven strategy of materials diversity does not require that production of the big two fibres should be stopped, but that alternative, more resource-efficient and culturally responsive fibres should be encouraged to flourish. Replacing some conventional cotton
Solution	production, for example, with alternatives such as organic or low-chemical cotton, flax, hemp and lyocell could bring benefits by reducing pesticide and water use. Likewise a shift from polyester to renewable and biodegradable fibres such as wool and those made from materials like corn starch could also bring benefits, reducing the dependency on oil. The result would be the cultivation, processing and promotion of a series of 'minority' fibres that, when taken together, amount to a majority. What is more, this majority has the potential not only to serve our material needs with reduced resource consumption, but it would also mean more varied and locally sensitive agriculture, more regional fibres, more local jobs, and more healthy and robust environments. Ideas about diversity rightly reflect the complexity of the relationship between fashion, textiles and sustainability. They underscore the importance of recognizing that no one fibre, regardless of whether it is organic, fairly traded or recycled, can single-handedly transform the practices of a polluting and resource-intensive industry into a more sustainable one. Indeed, a focus on materials alone is itself never likely to achieve this.

Task 5	Identifying the writer's purpose

It is important to identify what the writer's purpose is and his/her attitude to the topic. This helps you decide about the content and the extent to which it meets your needs. The final section of *Material diversity* contains a mixture of *explanation, exemplification, positive comment, negative criticism* and *suggestion.*

5.1 **Complete the annotation of the final section of Text 7a, reproduced below and on page 88.**

a. Re-read the text, paying close attention to the two annotations already made.

b. Locate, highlight and annotate other parts of the text that demonstrate the functions in the box below.

> explanation   exemplification (2 more)   negative criticism
>
> positive comment (1 more)   suggestion/recommendation (x 2)

c. Compare your annotations with another student's. Then compare them with a model your teacher will provide.

Annotations	Text
Positive comment	There are a range of different tools, software models and methods that can be used to examine the sustainability issues associated with the fibres used in modern fashion production. Some of these are based on qualitative assessments with the aim of gathering basic information about key issues; others quantify and balance a product's environmental impacts, frequently using a technique called 'life-cycle assessment'. These fibre assessment tools can be very valuable in driving forward new ideas and innovation in sustainable fashion design. They can do this by highlighting particularly polluting or resource-intensive practices, and so act as a spur to drive change towards low-impact methods and, when used as part of a creative process, to assess the sustainability potential of alternative scenarios and future strategies.
Exemplification	However, fibre assessments and comparisons have also been used in other ways, including defending a company's products, frequently shifting the spotlight of environmental impact onto other fibres (usually cotton). For example, in the early 1990s this strategy was adopted by the synthetic fibre producer DuPont. It published a ranking system of fibres which favoured polypropylene, followed by nylon, then wool, then polyester, acrylic and in sixth place – cotton (DuPont Environmental Excellence Team, 1999). Here,

Annotations	Text
	DuPont favoured synthetic fibres to its own benefit without revealing the assessment criteria being used, or the methodology upon which its research was based. In the same way, the cellulosic fibre producer Lenzing published 'research' which favoured its own viscose and lyocell fibres to the environmental detriment of cotton (Raninger, 1996, p. 74; Schmidtbauer, 1996).
	Cynically, these studies can be seen as an attempt to deflect scrutiny from these manufacturers' own products at a time when manufactured fibres were widely perceived as 'bad' for the environment. Yet these studies also hint at the beginnings of an awareness of a more complex and relational understanding of sustainability issues associated with textile fibres, and an understanding that has since been promoted by a wide range of other studies. Also the process of reviewing and comparing fibres creates opportunities to reduce the impact of unsustainable fibre use in the creation of modern fashion products. These include, for example, the development of better practices in the production of conventional fibres as well as the introduction of a group of different and inherently more ecologically sound fibres. Some of these changes could be brought about by a move to alternative systems of agriculture that are already well established – integrated pest management or organic cultivation methods, for example – while others are more challenging and need much further technical development.

Task 6 Producing a selective summary

The writer makes a number of recommendations and suggestions which should help alleviate the tensions which exist between the concepts of fashion and sustainability.

6.1 **Scan the text to identify which sections contain recommendations. Then complete the list of recommendations below.**

The first has been done for you; 3, 6 and 7 prompt you with the first part of the sentence.

The writer recommends:

1. having greater diversity _____

2. _____

3. *promoting ...* _____

4. _____

5. _____

6. *being aware of ...* _____

7. *developing better practices in ...* _____

8. _____

Text	Sustainable fashion, Text 7b (Source Book pp. 49–51)

Text 7b is from an article in *The Economist*, which further discusses issues related to the use of sustainable materials in the fashion industry.

Task 7	Before you read

You are now going to read Text 7b, which is more directly related to the topic of the clothing industry. One of your aims in reading this text is to compare the contents of this text with the first text (*Material diversity*). A second purpose is to identify examples from the text to support the idea that modern fashion can be sustainable, yet still attractive and desirable.

7.1 **Discuss the questions below.**
   1. In what ways have clothing fashions changed during your lifetime?
   2. How much do you consider environmental issues when shopping for clothes?

Task 8	Identifying the main ideas

8.1 **Read section headings 1–7 below and match them to Sections 1–6 in Text 7b.**
   Note: You will not need one of the headings.

Heading	Section
1. A more sustainable fur	
2. Popular now, but not in future?	
3. The most sustainable leather sources	
4. Unsustainable natural fur?	
5. Dilemmas facing customers	
6. Decline of North American wildlife	
7. The search for sustainable alternatives	

9.1   **Re-read Text 7b and answer the short-answer questions.**
This will help you differentiate between main and supporting points.

1. Why is it difficult for fashion to be sustainable?

    _____

2. What was apparently wrong with the sustainable-fashion style of the 1990s?

    _____

3. Which part of processing cotton causes the greatest pollution?

    _____

4. Why are organic cotton farmers criticized in this text?

    _____

5. What ecological disadvantages do bamboo and linen have as materials?

    _____

6. Identify a garment produced from recycled materials by Patagonia.

    _____

7. What can polyester now be transformed into because of modern advances?

    _____

8. Why have companies such as Tesco gained a good reputation with environmentalists?

    _____

9. Where in the USA has an important renewable leather industry developed?

    _____

10. What official verification of sustainability is being issued to customers buying such goods?

    _____

11. Which term in the text refers to fashion items which can be repaired?

    _____

12. Where does the vicuña originate from?

    _____

13. What do some clothing shops sell rather than muskrat or beaver furs?

    _____

14. Name the little-known source of fur mentioned by the writer.

    _____

15. To what extent are fashion designers taking note of sustainability issues? Find an appropriate expression in the text.

    _____

9.2 **Re-read the questions and your answers in Ex 9.1. Decide whether each question relates to a main or supporting point in terms of the overall text.**
Mark each question *M* (main) or *S* (supporting).

Task 10	Finding supporting information

Refer back to the Focus task on page 83. You should already have some ideas from Text 7a. You are now going to use Text 7b to make further notes that address the task.

10.1 **Identify the information and examples from Text 7b that support the ideas you already have for the Focus task.**
Note down key words with their line numbers, as shown in the example.

Supporting ideas	Line numbers
Patagonia – recycled plastic – fleeces	49–51

Text	The future of eco-fashion: A design-driven approach, Text 7c (Source Book pp. 52–54)

Text 7c is from a paper on the future of eco-design presented at a conference at the University of Oxford.

Task 11	Analyzing the title

In Units 4 and 5 you learnt that the title of a text can provide important insights into its content.

11.1 **Analyze the title of Text 7c to predict the probable content of the text.**
What two things can you deduce about the content?

_____

_____

_____

11.2   **Based on the title, think of questions the text might answer.**

Work with another student and write two or three questions. You will have a chance to compare these with alternative questions in a later task.

Does eco-fashion have a future?

| Task 12 | **Working out meaning from context** |

In earlier units, you have been working on deducing meaning from context (e.g., Unit 5, Text 5b, Task 10). It was explained that you need to use both language clues and logic to deduce the meaning. This task allows you to use logic, language and the preceding context.

12.1   **Decide where sentences a–g fit in Text 7c, following the steps below.**

Step 1: Read sentences a–g and highlight key words. These were all originally the final sentences of each of the seven paragraphs in the text you are going to read.

Step 2: Read through Text 7c. Decide which sentence (a–g) below belongs to each numbered gap (1–7) in the text.

Step 3: After making your decision, complete the table below by writing a–g in the appropriate column.

Step 4: Compare and discuss your answers with another student.

a.   Customers simply will not buy what is not appealing.

b.   In order to achieve this, eco-fashion needs to be not only driven by design but practised at every stage of the 'pipeline of product development' (Smal, 2008).

c.   Any claims to ecologically friendly developments in fashion creations, as with the fleece example, need to be carefully monitored to ensure that every stage in the process makes the item sustainable.

d.   Thus the T-shirt that consists of organic cotton must be designed and produced according to cleaner product principles to be ecologically acceptable.

e.   In other words, it is in the same danger as all fashion trends in that it could easily only have a limited lifespan.

f.   As a consequence, South African manufacturing might be forced to search globally for raw materials such as bamboo.

g.   As far as environmentally friendly fashion is concerned, these two categories should relate to each other while keeping the objective of eco-fashion in mind.

Position in text	1	2	3	4	5	6	7
Sentence letter							

Task 13	**Asking questions about the text**

13.1 **Look at the following questions and compare them with the ones you and other students wrote in Ex 11.2.**

a. Is it just the raw material which needs to be considered?
b. Are there different opinions about eco-fashion activities?
c. What is the key to producing all-round eco-friendly fashion?
d. What steps are involved in producing environmentally friendly clothes?
e. Why are eco-fashion garments so expensive?
f. What do most eco-aware customers look for?
g. What exactly is ecologically sound fashion?
h. How can the consumer identify environmentally friendly fashion?

Key skills: Asking questions of the text

If you ask questions and seek answers as you read, it will help you monitor your comprehension and ensure you do not lose sight of your reason for reading.

13.2 **Seven of the questions from Ex 13.1 are answered in Text 7c and one is not.**
Identify which paragraph most fully answers each question and complete the table below. The questions have been listed in a random order.

Paragraph	1	2	3	4	5	6	7
Question							

13.3 **To what extent do you think this text will help you complete the Focus task? Discuss your ideas with another student.**

Task 14	**Reading for a purpose**

We have already established the importance of reading for a purpose in Units 1 and 2. The three texts in this unit deal with issues of sustainable fashion; the reading purpose is introduced in the first text, *Material diversity*.

14.1 **Re-read the Focus task question and consider exactly what you are expected to do.**

 **FOCUS TASK** 👁

  The fashion industry poses a serious threat to the environment. A higher level of sustainability in materials production is the key solution. Discuss.

The first statement outlines a problem and the second suggests a solution. You are asked to discuss both of these statements. In other words, you are given an opportunity to:

■ decide to what extent you agree there is a problem
■ decide how far you feel the suggested solution is valid

In order to carry out this assignment, you must first find evidence to support your opinion. The texts you have read are intended to provide you with such evidence.

14.2 Re-read Text 7c and identify sections of the text that are relevant to the *problem* and sections that are relevant to the *solution*. Mark these either *P* or *S*.

14.3 Annotate the first three paragraphs below and then continue annotating in the margin of Text 7c.

As you annotate, also briefly summarize the main point in your own words, as in the examples.

Paragraph	Annotations
P1 The development of eco-fashion in the clothing industry is one of the most interesting lifestyle issues of the 21st century with some designers in the global and local fashion arenas creating their fashion collections around this concept. However, in recent discussions and debates on the concept, differing interpretations and endorsements of eco practices are emerging (Lee & Sevier, 2008). Clearly, though, for the fashion industry to be considered as environmentally friendly, it must have a positive effect on the environment and a measure of sustainability.	*S* The concept of sustainable fashion must be adhered to at every stage of production.
P2 For eco-fashion to be an effective contributor to the sustainability of the planet's present and future resources, it needs to continue to be a trend and also to become a best practice supported by all involved with the development and production of fashionable clothing. However, a definition of the term 'eco-fashion' is a necessary first step so that an acceptable set of criteria can be globally adopted. This can be clarified by considering what aspects in development and production eco-fashion should address. Firstly it needs to consist of products that are produced taking the environment into consideration. This could be achieved by a number of measures that can be grouped	

Paragraph	Annotations
into categories, namely (1) raw materials, components and processes and (2) production criteria and subsequent lifecycle. **P3** The selection of eco materials and how they are produced can have a significant influence on whether a fashion product can be considered an eco product or not. The components used in the production of an eco-fashion product, for example, could be organic in nature (such as using organic cotton) or recycled such as the well-known Patagonia model, where soda bottles are recycled for the production of fleece shirts. Similarly, the processes used in the manufacturing of an eco-fashion product need to adhere to sustaining the environment as opposed to using processes randomly without consideration of the detrimental effects these could have. Cleaner production methods applied during the development and manufacturing of materials all relate to this. Some examples are recycling of the wastewater used in dye houses and the use of energy when recycling soda bottles to generate the fibre needed for the fleece tops produced by Patagonia. Polyester can only be considered an eco-product if less energy is used in its production than in the development of natural polyester.	**P** Producers are not adhering to sustainable practice at every stage of production.

15.1 **Read the list of definitions in the table below and find a word or phrase in the text that matches each one.**

Scan the title and relevant paragraphs in Text 7c and identify the appropriate word or phrase.

Word or phrase	Paragraph	Definition
Clearly	1	unmistakably/plainly/without doubt
	title, 4, 6	motivated or directed
	2	a process that has been shown to work very effectively
	4	up to the present time or until now
	4	manufacturing goods in larger quantities using standardized designs
	4	work done by machines, automated
	4	attractive or desirable
	5	all-inclusive/complete
	5	something which creates an atmosphere of contentment or enjoyment
	6	very significant, important or influential
	7	common/frequent/established
	7	organization

15.2 **After you have finished, check your answers in a dictionary.**

Unit summary

Some new activities have been introduced in this unit. You have also had further practice in some activities that were introduced in the earlier units. The activities are listed below.

1 **Look back over the work you have done and think about how successfully you carried out the various tasks. As you are checking, tick (✔) the appropriate box in the table below.**

Skills and techniques	very well	quite well	need more work	not covered
Identifying main ideas				
Understanding the organization and function of sections in the text				
Identifying the writer's purpose				
Writing a 'selective' summary of specific information from a text				
Finding information to support ideas from a different text				
Asking questions about the text				
Identifying supporting information				

2 **Think about the following questions and try to write down an answer as briefly as possible. If you are unsure about an answer, discuss with another student and/or your teacher.**

a. Why is it important to analyze the title of a text before you begin reading it?

b. Why is it important to understand the writer's purpose before and while you are reading a text?

c. Why is it often necessary to read more than one text on a particular topic when undertaking academic study?

d. How can asking questions about a text before reading it help you achieve your reading purpose?

For web resources relevant to this unit, see:
www.englishforacademicstudy.com
These weblinks will provide you with further help with identifying the writer's pupose and working out meaning from context.

8 The Tipping Point

In this unit you will:

- analyze a text and use it to support your ideas
- become more aware of differences in academic style
- develop and consolidate the skills and strategies you learnt in previous units

Text	The Tipping Point: How Little Things Can Make a Big Difference, Text 8a (Source Book pp. 55–56)

Text 8a is an extract from *The Tipping Point* by Malcolm Gladwell. In *The Tipping Point*, Gladwell attempts to explain the changes and trends that occur in everyday life. He is particularly interested in why change often happens quickly and unexpectedly.

FOCUS TASK 👁

This assignment requires you to prepare a talk or write an essay on your impression of the main ideas developed by the author of *The Tipping Point*. You will do this by selecting appropriate information from Texts 8a–8d: an extract from the book, two reviews of the book and an interview with the author.

> Write a review of *The Tipping Point*. Briefly outline Gladwell's ideas and then express your opinion of his ideas.

Task 1	Reading and discussion

1.1 **The diagram below illustrates the concept of a tipping point. In pairs, discuss:**

1. the meaning of the diagram
2. what happens at the tipping point

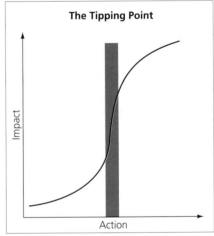

Source: Based on information from Gladwell, M. (2010). *The Tipping Point: How Little Things Can Make a Big Difference.* London: Abacus.

1.2   **Read the extract from the original text of *The Tipping Point*. Then discuss the following questions. Do not write answers at this point.**

1.   According to Gladwell, how can the emergence of an idea be compared to an epidemic?

_____

_____

2.   What do the sale of Hush Puppies and the decline in the New York crime rate have in common? Give three examples.

_____

_____

3.   How does Gladwell describe the changes that brought about the decline in the New York crime rate in paragraph 4?

_____

_____

4.   Identify the three incremental changes that occurred to mark the decline in New York criminal activities.

_____

_____

5.   Which of the three 'characteristics', according to Gladwell, is the most important?

_____

_____

6.   What happens when something reaches its tipping point?

_____

_____

1.3   **After you have discussed each question, make appropriate notes.**

1.4   **Look at the graph below. It is a *rough* illustration of criminal activities in the Brownsville and East New York areas during the period 1965–2000.**
   a.   Discuss what the graph shows.
   b.   Mark the tipping point on the graph.

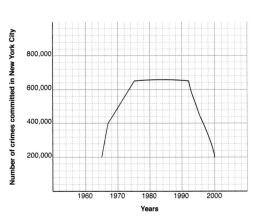

Source: Based on information from Gladwell, M. (2010). *The Tipping Point: How Little Things Can Make a Big Difference.* London: Abacus.

Text	Mental epidemics, Text 8b (Source Book pp. 57–59)

Text 8b is a review of *The Tipping Point* in *New Scientist*, which provides further insights into the ideas of Malcolm Gladwell.

Task 2	Pre-reading: Definitions

2.1 **Write a definition of the word *epidemic*.**

a.   Write your answer in no more than two sentences.

_____

_____

_____

_____

b.   Check your answer in a dictionary. To what extent is your definition the same?

2.2 **Read the following definition of an epidemic and answer the questions.**

Google | the influenza pandemic of 1918–19 |

Search   About 43,800 results (0.23 seconds)

The influenza pandemic of 1918–1919 killed more people than the Great War, known today as World War 1 (WW1), at somewhere between 20 and 40 million people. It has been cited as the most devastating epidemic in recorded world history. More people died of influenza in a single year than in four years of the Black Death Bubonic Plague from 1347 to 1351. Known as "Spanish Flu" or "La Grippe", the influenza of 1918–1919 was a global disaster.

Source: Billings, M. (2005). *The influenza pandemic of 1918*. Retrieved June 10, 2011, from Stanford University, Human Virology at Stanford website: http://stanford.edu/uda/

1.   Why do you think the Spanish Flu is referred to as both an epidemic and a pandemic?
2.   Can you think of any other epidemics? Make a list of examples.
3.   Are epidemics always related to illness and disease? Be prepared to explain your answer.

Task 3	Identifying functions of the text

This task will help you to identify the functions of different parts of a text written as a book review. It will help to familiarize you with the language used to comment on the ideas and opinions of a writer.

3.1 **Read Text 8b. As you read, decide which of the four main functions below best describes each paragraph.**

Complete row 2 of the table with the appropriate letter according to the function:
Explanation (**E**), Definition (**D**), Recommendations and advice (**R**), Comments and opinion (**C**)

Paragraph no.	1	2	3	4	5	6	7	8
Main purpose								

3.2 **Re-read the paragraphs you have marked *R* or *C* in the above table to indicate the writer's viewpoint.**

a. Highlight examples of words or phrases that make a positive, neutral or negative comment about Gladwell's book

b. Write them in the table below.

Paragraph no.	Words or phrases

Task 4	**Reading for specific information**

You have now read the text for the main idea and re-read parts of the text from the writer's viewpoint. You should now have a clear idea of the purpose of the text and be able to read quickly to answer specific questions.

4.1 **Re-read Text 8b and answer the following questions.**

Try to use as few words as possible in your answers, using note-form where appropriate. You will use your answers to write a summary of the text later in the unit.

1. What type of epidemics does Gladwell's book refer to?

_____

2. When is the tipping point reached?

_____

3. What adverbs does Marsden use to indicate that he agrees with Gladwell to some extent?

_____

4. What epidemic occurred in Micronesia in the 1970s?

_____

5. Explain the phrase 'The Next Big Thing'.

_____

6. Which publication did Gladwell write for?

_____

7. How many stages are involved in Gladwell's process?

_____

8. What theory does Gladwell have for people not believing in the simplicity of his ideas?

_____

9. What is important in order to achieve a full-scale epidemic?

_____

10. Which means of crimeprevention is mentioned in the text?

_____

11. What experiment is mentioned?

_____

12. Richard Dawkins is associated with:

_____

13. What is Gladwell campaigning against in the concluding part of his book?

_____

14. What is the source of this text?

_____

Task 5   Dealing with unfamiliar words

There are a number of low-frequency or less common words in Text 8b. As a result, you may find it difficult to guess their meaning. In previous units, you have seen that identifying the word class of an unfamiliar word and looking at the context in which the word occurs can help you to work out its meaning. The tasks below provide further practice in this key skill.

5.1 **Match the definitions to the appropriate word classes given in the table on the next page. Write the corresponding number for the relevant definitions in row 2.**

1. describes an action

2. describes a thing, quality, situation or person

3. usually comes before a noun or pronoun, showing its relation to another part of a sentence

4. refers to a person or a thing

5. describes an adjective, verb or adverb

6. replaces or refers to a noun

Word class	noun	pronoun	verb	adjective	adverb	preposition
Definition						

Key reading skills: Guessing words from function

One approach to working out the meaning of an unknown word or phrase is to identify the 'function' it has in a sentence or phrase. For example, in Paragraph 1 of Text 8b you may not recognize the meaning of one of the words in the phrase *the latest craze, fad or fashion* (line 6). However, you can see that all three words (*craze, fad, fashion*) are nouns; they also appear to have a similar meaning because they are closely linked. In this case, if you know the word *fashion*, you can probably work out that *craze* and *fad* have similar meanings. A good reader would probably not concern themselves with investigating further, as they would already have an approximate understanding.

5.2 **Work out the meanings of the words in the table below. Follow the procedure below.**

a. Locate each word in the text and identify its word class. Complete column 2 of the table.

b. Look for clues in the surrounding context to help you to guess the meaning of each word. Complete column 3.

c. Compare your answers with another student's. Work together to think of a possible synonym (word or short phrase) for each word and complete column 4. Remember that the synonym must be the same word class and be able to replace the original word in the context.

d. Check meanings and synonyms in a dictionary, if necessary.

The first one has been done as an example.

Word in text	Word class	Meaning in context	Possible synonym
threshold	noun	the point at which something starts happening	starting point
demanding			
plummeted			
seemingly			
relevant			
workable			
context			
reference			
whereby			

Task 6 — Analyzing the writer's choice of expression

The style of writing in reviews in popular publications tends to be less formal than in academic texts. They usually contain many *colloquial* and *idiomatic* expressions to make the writing more colourful and interesting for the reader. However, the use of such words and expressions can cause problems for language learners because meaning is not always immediately predictable. This task highlights some of these words and expressions in Text 8b, and encourages you to think about their meanings in context and the effect they have on the reader.

6.1 **Re-read Paragraph 3 in Text 8b and think about how the writer uses the eight words and phrases below.**

    a. Locate each word or phrase in the text and try to work out its meaning in context.

    b. Think of the effect the writer's use of language has on the reader.

    c. Discuss your ideas with another student.

        1. squiggle-babble

        2. the masses

        3. by the force of word of mouth

        4. to keep up with the Joneses

        5. snowball

        6. a cosmetic makeover

        7. tweak and test

        8. hunter-gatherer past

6.2 **Check your answers by reading the following sentences in which the word or phrase has been used.**

Some are used in a similar way to the text, but others have a more literal meaning, showing the origins of the word or phrase.

1. I couldn't understand a word she said, it was all squiggle-babble to me!

2. Thousands of people came en masse to demonstrate against the price rises.

3. Very few people could read in those days, so information was passed by word of mouth.

4. The Jones family always seem to have bought the latest things.

5. As the snowball rolled down the hill, it got bigger and bigger.

6. Looking in the mirror, she could see that the cosmetic makeover had made her look much younger.

7. The essay needed a few slight changes. A little tweaking and it would be perfect.

8. Early man survived by hunting animals and gathering fruit.

Task 7 — Writing a selective summary

A useful way of deconstructing a question is to write it out again in your own words. This may help you to decide what notes you need to make.

7.1 **Look carefully at the following question. Then rewrite it in your own words.**
To what extent does the writer of this text, Paul Marsden, feel that *The Tipping Point* is a book worth reading?

_____

_____

_____

_____

7.2 **Write a short paragraph summarizing Marsden's opinion of *The Tipping Point*.**
a. Look back at Tasks 3 and 4 and decide what information from these two tasks will help you to write the summary.
b. Re-read the text, if necessary, and annotate the passages that show the writer's opinions.
c. Make notes and use them to write the paragraph.
d. Use words from the box below where appropriate.

on the whole	however	in general	throughout the review
furthermore		overall	in many instances

Text	**An interview with Malcolm Gladwell, Text 8c** (Source Book pp. 60–62)

Text 8c is an interview with the author of *The Tipping Point*, Malcolm Gladwell. The views he expresses may assist your understanding of the extract from the book (Text 8a) and the review (Text 8b).

Task 8	Identifying main ideas

You are going to read an interview with Malcolm Gladwell, in which he explains the ideas presented in his book. This task will provide further practice in identifying key ideas in the text.

8.1 **Read the interview questions 1–8 on page 106 and follow the steps below.**
a. Read the questions and underline key words.
b. Try to predict the order in which the questions are asked and discuss your predictions with a partner.
c. Read the text to match the questions with the appropriate response by Gladwell in the text on pages 60–62 of the Source Book. (There is one extra question which is not asked.)
d. Compare your answers with your partner. How successful were you at predicting the order of the questions?

1. What do you hope readers will learn from the book?

2. Why do you think the epidemic example is so relevant for other kinds of change? Is it just that it's an unusual and interesting way to think about the world?

3. Are you talking about the idea of memes that has become so popular in academic circles recently?

4. What is *The Tipping Point* about?

5. Why did you write the book? Was it because of your experience as a news reporter?

6. Where did you get the idea for the book?

7. How would you classify *The Tipping Point*? Is it a science book?

8. What does it mean to think about life as an epidemic? Why does thinking in terms of epidemics change the way we view the world?

8.2 **Re-read each of Gladwell's responses to the questions.**
   a. Within each response, find and underline a sentence that you think best summarizes the answer to each question.
   b. Compare your ideas with a partner's and discuss any differences.

   Example:
   What is *The Tipping Point* about?

   The Tipping Point is an examination of the social epidemics that surround us. (the last sentence in the response)

8.3 **There is a lot of vocabulary in the text related to disease, e.g., *epidemic*, *measles*, etc. Scan the text and highlight as many examples as you can find.**

8.4 **Compare your findings with other students. Then decide whether any of these words would be useful for you to know in the future and, if so, record them.**

8.5 **Discuss why diseases and other medical terms are used in *The Tipping Point*.**

Text	*The Tipping Point* by Malcolm Gladwell: Book review, Text 8d (Source Book pp. 63–65)

Text 8d is another review of *The Tipping Point,* which will provide further insights into the nature of Gladwell's ideas.

Task 9	Short-answer questions

You are going to read another review of Gladwell's book. Later you will use some of the information to prepare a talk or write an essay about *The Tipping Point*.

First, you will have a final opportunity to check your ability to read quickly. As already mentioned, it is important to read texts as quickly as possible to get a general idea about their content. It is essential to get at least a superficial understanding of the text no matter how quickly you are reading. Without gaining some understanding with your first reading, you will not have achieved your reading purpose.

9.1   **Read the text as quickly as you can and then answer the questions.**
Time yourself to see how long it takes. There are 1,396 words in this text.

a.   Answer as many questions as you can without looking back at the text. Then discuss your answers with a partner – again without reading the text.

b.   Next check your answers by looking at the text and correcting any answers which you got wrong, or completing answers you were unable to attempt.

1.   'The straw that broke the camel's back' is the same idea as …

_____

2.   Where did the nurse first hold her seminars?

_____

3.   Where did she hold her seminars next?

_____

4.   What was the final result of moving locations?

_____

5.   Name the three kinds of people Gladwell describes?

_____

6.   Which characters from Sesame Street are mentioned?

_____

7.   In the Stanford University psychological study, students were divided into two groups. What were these groups?

_____

8.   Who shot four muggers on a subway in 1984?

_____

9.   What did David Gunn do when he was subway director?

_____

10.   What did William Bratton do to reduce crime rates on the subway?

_____

9.2   **Think about how well you understood the text from the first reading as well as the time it took you to read the text.**
What strategies might you use to improve your reading speed and understanding? List some ideas and discuss them with other students.

Task 10   Understanding general ideas in the text

There are six sections in this review. Each section answers a question asked by the writer, Bill Cattey.

10.1   **Read through each section again and decide which of the following questions is answered in each section.**

There is one extra question which is not answered.

a. What motivated Gladwell to write *The Tipping Point*?
b. How is a tipping point achieved?
c. How does Cattey justify the book as a good read?
d. What is a tipping point?
e. Why did Cattey care about what was in the book?
f. What did Gladwell learn from working with younger people?
g. Why do tipping points occur?

Section	1	2	3	4	5	6
Question						

Task 11   Academic style

The review by Bill Cattey is not only worth studying for the content, but because of the language and style he uses.

11.1   **Look at the introduction and first paragraph and comment on the language and style.**

Would you say the style is academic? Give reasons for your answer.

11.2   **Study the sentence beginning *Gladwell studies* … (line 19).**

There is some useful academic language in this sentence, i.e., language that you could use in your own academic texts. For example, *Gladwell studies several cases in detail and verifiable evidence.*

11.3   **Find more sentences and phrases beginning *Gladwell* … Underline further examples of academic language that might be useful.**

This language could be useful in your own writing or at least help you in your reading.

11.4   **Discuss your highlighted examples with another student and/or your teacher.**

Unit summary

Some new activities have been introduced in the final unit. You have also had further practice in activities that were introduced in earlier parts of the book. The activities are listed below.

1 **Look back over the work you have done and think about how successfully you carried out the various tasks. As you check, tick (✔) the appropriate box in the table below.**

Skills and techniques	very well	quite well	need more work	not covered
Investigating a definition				
Identifying the function of the text				
Identifying the writer's viewpoint				
Analyzing the writer's choice of expression				
Dealing with unfamiliar words				
Writing a selective summary				
Finding specific examples of academic language				

2 **Read the text that follows and complete the gaps with words from the box. Two of these words are not appropriate and should not be used.**

range	whereas	academic	examples	use
frequency	rarely	number	technical	speakers

High-_____ words are those in most common use in either the written

or spoken language, or in both, by the whole _____ of native and

non-native _____ of a language. Low-frequency words, however,

tend to be _____ or related to a specific area of study. For example,

applied linguists tend to write or talk about 'discourse analysis' or 'transformational

grammar', _____ even very well-educated non-applied linguists

would _____, if ever, use such terms because they require specialist

knowledge to do so. For international students, deciding whether to record, learn

and _____ a word may, to a certain extent, depend on their area of

study. However, there is a large number of words or phrases which are used in general

_____ language and would be common across academic disciplines.

Examples include: *with reference to*; *the evidence suggests that*; *conversely,* etc.

For web resources relevant to this book, see:
www.englishforacademicstudy.com

These weblinks will provide you with further information on analyzing the author's choice of expression and on dealing with unfamiliar words.

Glossary

active vocabulary
Vocabulary that you use in your day-to-day life in order to communicate effectively.

annotate
To write comments or explanatory notes directly onto a text, e.g., in the margin.

careful reading
Reading slowly and carefully to develop a clear understanding of the text or a particular part of the text. For example, you would read carefully to understand details or to infer meaning.

complex sentences
Sentences that are made up of several clauses (main and dependent clauses). They may also include long phrases or unusual syntax and/or terminology.

displayed information
Information that is displayed in and around a text, such as headings and titles, text boxes, tables, graphs and diagrams. Displayed information, also known as *overt information*, often highlights key words and ideas.

foreword
A section of a book or longer text that comes at the beginning and gives a short introduction to it. This introduction is often written by someone other than the author and may be in the form of a short essay.

infer (v)
To obtain or work out meaning from the text that the writer has not explicitly stated. This is sometimes called 'reading between the lines' and involves the reader making use of his or her world knowledge.

paragraph leader
The first sentence in a written paragraph. The paragraph leader links to the ideas in the previous paragraph and may lead into the ideas in the next paragraph. The paragraph leader can sometimes also be a topic sentence.

predicting
The skill of using what you already know and what you want to know about a topic to guess what the text will contain. Clues such as titles, pictures, layout and paragraph leaders can help you predict and make the text less challenging to read or difficult to understand.

previewing
Looking at text to decide how useful it is for a particular purpose. Previewing might involve looking at: the contents page, the foreword or introduction and/or the index.

prior knowledge
This is knowledge that you already have about something, sometimes known as *general knowledge* or *world knowledge*. If you have prior knowledge of key vocabulary, or an idea in a text (e.g., from reading about it in your own language), you will generally find the text easier to follow.

reading critically
Reading in a way that involves questioning what the text says, what the writer is trying to do and how he or she does this, e.g., whether the text is biased or prejudiced.

reading for a purpose
Having a specific reason for reading a text, e.g., reading to learn, reading for entertainment or reading to confirm. The reading purpose will affect which reading strategy to apply, e.g., fast skimming, browsing, search-reading, intensive reading.

read selectively
Selective reading involves choosing certain sections in a text to read carefully because these are the areas that you wish to understand or research in more depth. You read selectively when you have a clear purpose for reading.

reading strategy
Something that you can actively do to help your reading or improve your reading skills over a period of time. Typical reading strategies for academic texts include: knowing your reading purpose, picking out key words and note-taking.

recall
Remembering information and/or ideas from a text that you have read, to help you in your own writing.

references
Acknowledgement of the sources of ideas and information used or mentioned in a text. References allow a reader to check those sources for accuracy or to find out more information about the topic.

scanning
Reading for specific information involves scanning. It involves finding key words or figures. For example, it is normal to scan a text to find dates, names and specific facts.

search reading
Looking through a text quickly to find specific *ideas* rather than *words*. It is different from scanning because you do not know the specific words you are looking for.

skimming
Reading for the general idea or gist of a text involves skimming – reading the text quickly to get the main idea of what it is about rather than focusing on every word. For example, it is normal to skim a letter or book cover to find out what it is about. This often precedes reading for more specific information.

supporting sentences
Sentences that follow or support the main idea or topic sentence in a paragraph. Supporting sentences may give examples, explanations or additional information about the key idea.

synthesize
To take information from different sources and to write it all up as a single text.

text analysis
Checking the currency, authorship, purpose, accessibility, relevance and interest value of a text.

topic sentence
A sentence that carries the main idea of the paragraph. It often comes at the beginning or end of a paragraph, but may also appear elsewhere. It is usually followed by supporting sentences or preceded by them. There may be more than one topic sentence in a paragraph or none at all.

word class
Words can be grouped into classes according to their function in a sentence. Word classes, also known as parts of speech, include *nouns*, *verbs*, *adjectives* and *adverbs*.